MEG WESTLEY

A CHILD'S YEAR IN PARIS, 1963

◆ FriesenPress

Suite 300 - 990 Fort St
Victoria, BC, V8V 3K2
Canada

www.friesenpress.com

ISBN
978-1-5255-6817-6 (Hardcover)
978-1-5255-6818-3 (Paperback)
978-1-5255-6819-0 (eBook)

1. BIOGRAPHY & AUTOBIOGRAPHY, PERSONAL MEMOIRS

Distributed to the trade by The Ingram Book Company

To Laura,
Ah, Paris!
Ooh la la & bon voyage!
xx

Milk with WINE

meg Westley

For

Neil and Frances, who shared the journey

and my children

Jamie, Mike, CA, and Aaron

Preface

This is the story of the year I spent in Paris in 1963–4, a long time ago. Lacking a photographic memory, I cannot recall conversations verbatim, and have used artistic license in fleshing out many of the details of the story. My brother and sister may have quite different recollections of the events described here, if they remember them at all. Such is the nature of memory.

Nonetheless, I was surprised, when I started writing the book, at how vividly some incidents and details came back to me. It was a unique year in my life.

The first names of my young French friends are correct, as are all place names in the book. I revisited 'my' school in 2017, to speak with the current principal, in hopes of obtaining the full names of my classmates and possibly contacting them. The principal was too busy to see me. Some things never change. The school itself looks much as it did in 1964, as does the house where we lived at 6 rue Nicolet (at least from the outside).

1

Lunatic Child

As the music soared from the record player, I danced an achingly delicate rendition of *Swan Lake*. Ever since seeing the ballet, I'd devoted hours to re-enacting the tragic tale. I flapped my swan wings and sailed through the air. At age eight, I knew I was destined to be a ballerina. It was January 1963.

The record stopped abruptly, and I stumbled in a less-than-swan-like way.

"Come on down everyone," shouted my father. "We have big news."

My mother stood in the doorway, grinning.

I plopped onto the couch. Frances and Neil scrambled down the stairs. When we'd all gathered, my father announced, "Next year is my sabbatical and we're going to Paris to live for a year."

The world of dying swans dimmed. I had no idea what a sabbatical was, but Paris!

My teenaged sister and brother shouted questions.

1

"A whole year? What about school?" Frances cared a lot about school.

"Are the girls there as sexy as they say?"

"Neil!" my mother reprimanded.

"How will we get there?" Frances asked. "What about my friends?"

"It's going to be a great adventure," said my father.

The next day I slid along the icy sidewalk, bundled in my snowsuit, eager to tell my friend Jenny. We lived on the main street of Montreal West. Jenny lived halfway to school.

"We're going to Paris," I sang out when I saw her waiting for me on the porch.

Jenny frowned as she descended the steps. "Where?"

"Paris! The most beautiful city in the world. It's very romantic and full of intellectuals." I used my parents' words. They thought highly of intellectuals. My father was a professor at McGill.

"Why do you want to go there?" asked Jenny.

"Because it will be an adventure!" I said, but her question gave me pause. Did I really want to spend a year so far from my home?

"Sounds weird to me," Jenny said. She thought my whole family was weird because my parents were American. Jenny said they talked funny, like when Dad said "ruff" instead of "roof." Jenny said even I talked funny, because I read a lot and knew big words.

I stuck my tongue out at her, but her words made me think. What would Paris be like? I didn't know much about big cities. I'd only been to downtown Montreal a few times. I knew almost nothing about Paris, but I wasn't going to let Jenny know that.

Over the next months, we all bombarded my parents with questions, though often I felt too exhausted to care. I'd been ill off and on for over a year; I had little appetite and often ran a fever on weekends. My mother trotted me from doctor to doctor trying to figure out what was wrong. They shook their heads and suggested removing my perfectly healthy tonsils. My mother realized the fevers occurred when I was tired. Her solution was to make me stay in bed on the weekends, which seemed grossly unfair. I didn't feel that bad, why couldn't I go out and play like other kids? She bribed me with unlimited in-bed television and macaroni and cheese. Watching *The Avengers*, I imagined myself as Emma Peel doing karate and almost forgot what I was missing outside. Despite my mother's efforts, I lost weight. I looked like a stick figure, all bony limbs, with dark circles under my eyes. Still, my peculiar illness wasn't about to get in the way of the big plans.

In July, we boarded a Cunard Line ship and set off for England. The ship had a huge dining room, shops, vast decks, and cabins with round windows. I took the role of intrepid adventurer—a character from one of Enid Blyton's Adventure books. I'd peek around corners looking for pirates and then launch myself up the steep staircases, clinging to the railings as the ship lurched. I particularly liked the indoor pool. Such a curious idea, a pool full of water in the depths of a floating ship. Sort of like those Russian stacking dolls. Even when they closed the pool in rough weather, I'd stand at the glass door gazing in. As the ship heaved, all the water crashed to one end of the pool, revealing the bottom at the other end.

The rest of the family did nothing but eat and complain about getting fat. I couldn't understand this. As I had virtually no appetite, the mounds of food presented at every meal held no appeal for me. But the costume ball, with prizes, sent me frantic with excitement. My brother and sister went as Romans, in towels and costume jewellery. I took the role of a princess. In nightgown and bangles, I cut quite the figure. I should have won the prize.

We landed in England, where people spoke in old-fashioned ways. Castles rose at every corner; we rode on double-decker buses and saw the crown jewels, the Tower of London, and London Bridge. We took the Underground and watched plays in gilt theatres. After seeing *The Mousetrap*, I decided when I grew up, I'd write plays like Agatha Christie.

And yet, one cathedral looked much like another. I soon came to loathe museums and art galleries. The restaurant food made me queasy: steak and kidney pies, bangers and mash, fish and chips. It all dripped with grease and exuded unpleasant odours.

Worst of all, I had no one to play with. I was sick of doing *adult* stuff. I longed for friends my own age, other children.

One day, just for fun, I threw a fit, scrunched up my face like a lunatic, sprawled on the sooty London sidewalk, rolled my eyes and made gurgling noises. My parents' eyes grew large and their faces loomed over me. "Are you all right? Meg? MEG!"

I burst into laughter. They dragged me to my feet, tight-lipped, and we continued on to the next dreary historical site. Delighted by their reaction, I repeated this performance over and over again while everyone screamed at me to *Stop that and behave yourself.* No sooner did I lurch and grimace than my sister would retreat, horrified by the thought that anyone might associate me with her. I enjoyed every minute of it, especially my family's discomfort. It served them right for dragging me to all these stupid places.

Perhaps in an effort to entertain me, my parents took us to see movies ("films" the Brits said). My sister sobbed over the star-crossed lovers in *West Side Story.* Afterwards, my brother adopted a swagger and a Jets-style accent. I belted out an off-tune version of *Amer-ee-ca,* stamped my feet, and wished I had a brightly coloured skirt like Anita.

One warm summer night, we took the Underground to Regent's Park to see *A Midsummer Night's Dream.* When the sun set, fairyland appeared. Tiny magical lights adorned the marble staircase; fairies flitted; a funny man called Bottom turned into a donkey, and the boys all fell in love with the small dark girl (like me!) instead of the tall blonde. I sat wide-eyed, late into the night. The next day I announced a change of plans. I would not be a ballerina or a writer. I'd be an actress!

When I was not behaving like a lunatic, people thought I was cute: the owners of the Bed and Breakfast where we stayed, waitresses, tour guides, pub owners, and especially a family named Williams with whom we stayed near Oxford. I liked the Williams because they had children. They lived in an old house in the countryside, with horses but no cathedrals in sight. The daughter Kate was a few years older than me. She rode horses, so I decided I wanted to learn to ride, even though I was neither fond of big animals, nor very athletic. The Williams approved heartily and persuaded my parents to let me stay with them an extra week. I doubt it took much persuading.

I did not take well to horseback riding. The enormous creatures terrified me, and I didn't get to wear a fancy costume like Kate. I loved her tall riding boots and velvet hard hat, but they had nothing like that for me and soon my enthusiasm for the whole project waned. Still, I basked in the affection of Mrs. Williams, despite the faint aroma of horse dung that clung to her.

I enjoyed being away from my family. For two days. Then it started to rain. Mist blurred the green landscape. I lost all interest in outdoor activities, and England generally. Why couldn't these people talk proper English? Why did they have to say the W.C. when they meant the bathroom, crisps when they meant chips, jumpers instead of sweaters? Why was the toilet so cold and the long chain so hard to reach? I was greatly relieved when my parents finally drove up to collect me.

They'd bought a white Volkswagen when we arrived in England. Planning to drive it all year, they'd chosen a car designed to be driven on the right-hand side of the road and my father had manfully, but not always successfully, struggled to drive on the left in England.

On the trip back from the Williams' farm, my father grinned and said, "I think I've finally got the hang of this."

Just then a truck hurtled directly at us on the narrow road.

"Bill!" my mother shrieked.

He swerved to the left side of the road, where we should have been, just in time to avoid a head-on collision. It was definitely time to leave England.

On the ferry from Dover to Le Havre, my excitement grew. Soon we'd be in Paris, the city of my parents' dreams! I suspected they'd fallen in love *because* of Paris. My mother had told me the story a million times.

They'd met at the University of Chicago. On their first date, my father spent a month's rent taking Mom to a fancy dance club. He bought a bottle of champagne. By mistake, she kicked it over. He managed not to sob aloud as the precious champagne poured out on the floor. She found him charming.

Later that night, walking under the moonlight, they talked about Paris, city of artists, writers, and romance. One day, they promised each other, they would go to Paris and live *la vie en rose*, which meant a rosy life.

2

Louie Cans and the View

We got to Paris alive, despite the insane French drivers who honked and raced past us on the highway from Le Havre. My father muttered a steady stream of curses; my mother alternately shrieked in terror and scolded him for his language. When we reached the city limits, the traffic slowed but became more terrifying. We circled round and round a massive roundabout with six lanes for traffic, and drivers behaving as though there were ten (according to my outraged mother). We all craned to see street signs while French drivers bellowed at us every time we slowed. It felt like hours before we arrived at our destination.

The hotel looked pretty much like every other building on the street, except for the faded sign; the door opened directly onto the street and paint peeled on the window shutters. As we emerged from the car, the smell of Paris enveloped me: a potent combination of garlic, French tobacco, and urine. Other scents drifted in and out: fresh baking from the *boulangeries*, pungent cheeses and sausages from the *fromageries* and *epiceries*, wine, coffee, and cigarette smoke from the cafes and *tabacs*. I found the city's distinctive odor exotic and disgusting.

The first few weeks we stayed in the Latin Quarter. I don't know why they called it Latin, since everyone spoke French. I had somehow failed to anticipate this disturbing development. I knew people in France spoke French, but all the time?

Though hardly splendid, the hotel was still a thrill. *We're in a hotel. We're in a hotel.* The desk clerk seemed snooty, ignoring my parents' questions, but I liked the tiny elevator with barred doors that clanked up to our floor. I roamed our high-ceilinged room and peered out tall windows onto the bustling street, bounced on the narrow bed, and examined the toilet-that-wasn't-quite-a-toilet. (My mother, blushing, called it a *beeday*.)

However, the room, in the end, was just a room, and rather confining. We went for walks. I was shocked to learn that the urine smell came from the urinals (*pissoires*) that adorned most of the city's avenues and boulevards. While some were lovely little buildings with filigree decorations, I found the stench and the brazenness of men ducking in to use these street outhouses pretty repulsive.

Within two days, boredom set in again. My parents, who seemed perpetually distracted, did not take us to plays or films, or do anything much to entertain us.

"There's nothing to do," I wailed.

Of course, my parents had larger concerns: negotiating in broken French to obtain lodging for the year and school-ing for their three children. My father trudged the streets by day seeking accommodation, while my mother kept an eye on us. Sometimes they went out together and left my older siblings in charge. Soon we were all moaning, "When will we get out of this hotel?"

One day my parents returned in a state of agitation. My father's eyes gleamed. My mother had a worried crease in her forehead and unusual colour in her cheeks.

"We really can't afford it." My father looked up from a pad on which he'd been scribbling.

"You're right. We'll keep looking." My mother's mouth drooped.

"But Montmartre," my father sighed.

They gazed at each other dreamily.

"There are too many antiques," my mother said, shaking her head. "The children would break them. And the damage deposit. It's just too much."

"You're right." My father frowned. "It's far more than we've budgeted for."

This conversation continued over several days as they resumed their search. School would begin soon; they had to get us settled.

"Meg's school would be just around the corner," said my mother.

"And the view." My father's voice had a faraway quality.

"But it would mean a long metro ride for Neil and Frances. To reach the American school."

"Too long, do you think?"

My mother wavered. "Maybe not. I mean, they'd go together. They are teenagers."

They'd found a small house, in *Montmartre*, they said in awed tones, as though it were Narnia. The house had A View, apparently a critical detail. A View Over the Rooftops of Paris. But it was horribly expensive and full of Louie Cans furniture. I didn't know Louie Cans, but gathered his furniture was so delicate that Neil and I would splinter it all in a matter of minutes. The tall, narrow house had one room on the ground floor, two small bedrooms on the second and a single living room-kitchen at the top. One minute my parents decided it was too small, would feel cramped, had too many stairs. The next they thought it charming and quaint, quintessentially Parisian.

In the end, they did rent the house at *6 rue Nicolet* in the 18th *arrondissement (Montmartre)* for the year. We arrived at the tiny street on a bright fall morning. The fierce landlady, Madame Dufrèche, met us at the door. After a long discussion, in which she spoke in loud, firm tones and my mother nodded and smiled, saying "We, we, we," Madame sniffed, handed over the keys and swept away.

The house featured a half-door entrance for the housekeeper, whom Madame Dufrèche insisted we hire. On discovering this small door, I felt like I'd entered Wonderland. Everyone else thought it degrading that the housekeeper should have to practically crawl into the house, but I could pass through the little door by just ducking my head! The courtyard behind our house, with doors leading to other dwellings, also intrigued me. It was dank and smelly but also somehow mysterious, hidden as it was from the street.

My sister and I shared a small bedroom with a three-quarter bed and sausage-like pillow roll that looked grand, the sort of thing we'd seen in castle bedrooms, but turned out to be uncomfortable. By order of Madame Dufrèche, metal folding shutters over the windows had to be closed nightly, even on the second floor, to prevent break-ins. Given that we'd never even locked our front door in Montreal West, I found this very odd. But Madame Dufrèche clearly had some sort of hold over my parents; they obeyed her every directive to the letter.

The Louie Cans furniture also reminded me, for good reason, of the stuff we'd seen in castles—and were to see much more of in the French *chateaux*. Beautiful items, if spindly and old, adorned the entire house. (In time I realized that *quinze* was actually the French word for fifteen, and that Louis XV was an old dead king who liked fancy furniture.) Even I appreciated the View. The house stood partway up the southeastern side of Montmartre. Windows covered one whole wall of the top floor, flooding the room with light and looking out over a patchwork of rooftops as far as the eye could see. I loved the house. Small, full of funny features, a bit like a dollhouse, it was a perfect place to pretend to be a fairy or a Borrower. The only downside was my mother constantly telling us to "be careful." We tiptoed around, trying not to touch anything.

In the early morning, trucks honked and beeped, and men shouted right outside our shuttered window. We quickly got to know the neighbourhood: the *boulangerie* at the bottom of the street where we bought hot baguettes every morning, and many other shops, each specializing in a certain type of food, so different from the big grocery stores at home. I loitered outside the shops, gazing at the displays. One window featured mouth-watering pastries, cakes, and little tarts, with glazed strawberry or rich dark chocolate toppings. Other shop windows held hundreds of cheeses, although not the orange cheddar that I loved. Slippery mounds of shrimps and eels and other disgusting creatures tainted the air with fishy smells outside one store. At another, fresh slabs of meat, whole chickens, and bins of scary-looking grisly bits sat right next to a pig's head. I turned away, repulsed, only to stare into the next window where radish curlicues decorated shredded carrot salads and glazed pates. While I found much of the food revolting, I admired the way the shopkeepers presented their wares.

Twice a week we walked a few blocks to the local market where row upon row of stalls held brightly coloured fruits, vegetables, and flowers. My mother bargained bravely with the stall-keepers. They sniffed at her accent, but accepted her *francs* and *centimes*, and we crammed our purchases into the stretchy string bags carried by French housewives. The first time we arrived at the market, the merchants simply shrugged at my mother's request for a bag, as though she were a cretin.

Despite the challenges, my parents were thrilled.

"Just as Hemingway described," they murmured as they hustled us into chairs at an outdoor café. They sipped wine and I dug into a fancy ice cream. Young women on bicycles with baguettes strapped to their backs chimed bells as they rode past. Next to us, grizzled old men drank coffee and a murky yellow liquid that smelled like licorice. The September sun warmed the grey buildings and reflected off windows with narrow wrought-iron balconies. Cobblestone streets, ancient buildings, wide boulevards, trees with fili-greed gratings embedded in the sidewalk around them, the exotic air—all of it seemed magical.

Only two things troubled me: I had no friends, and no one spoke English.

"Don't you fret, honey." My mother smiled. "As soon as you start school, you'll make lots of friends."

"But I won't be able to talk to them! How can I make friends when I can't speak French?"

She laughed. "Meg, you'll be speaking fluently in no time. Honest."

I laughed too, cheered by her optimism. All would be well.

3

Madame la Maîtresse

My mother had researched the local school and arranged to enrol me there. It was about three blocks from our house. The principal, my mother assured me, couldn't wait for me to arrive. I could come home at lunch, unlike my siblings, who had a long metro ride to their school. On the other hand, they would be with American classmates. I would have happily sacrificed home-cooked lunch for English-speaking friends.

On a cool fall morning, my mother brushed my hair and dressed me in a skirt and blouse. We trotted down our little street and around a corner onto a large boulevard. At the end of the block stood an imposing stone building: my new school.

I'd always liked school. Education was a sort of religion in our house, the one absolute expectation being that we'd all achieve well. I had always done so. I enjoyed getting teacher approval and, for the most part, learning. Clutching my mother's hand, I tried to tell myself this was just another school and I'd do fine.

We passed through a doorway marked *Filles* into a large interior courtyard. Open corridors ran around all four sides; off them, doors led to the classrooms. The courtyard contained a crowd of chattering girls, all wearing little coloured coats like the white ones doctors wear. I felt a flicker of panic. I had no such coat.

My mother led me to a classroom. She handed me over to *Madame la Maîtresse,* a forbidding woman with sharp features and stern eyes.

Then she abandoned me.

I knew I'd been put back a year, so would be retaking Grade Two, because of my lack of French. Looking around at the little girls, I realized that not only did I not have the required smock, I also stood out because—for the first (and last) time in my life—I was taller than most of my classmates.

Madame examined me as though I were an insect and gabbled at me incomprehensibly. Feeling a little embarrassed for her, I tried to explain that I did not speak French. She took me by the shoulder, hustled me to a desk near the back of the room, and plunked me down in the seat. She paused, looked me over, and gabbled again. I tried to smile, but my face felt frozen. She gave a great sigh, stalked over to some hooks on the wall, took down a grey smock and tossed it to me.

The girls sniggered. I flushed and pulled on the smock. Old and too large for me, it was nothing like the brightly coloured, well-fitting smocks worn by the other girls.

Madame made announcements. The little girls opened books and, to my horror, dipped nib pens into inkpots and began to write. I opened the book before me and stared at the inkpot, never having seen a nib pen before. The girl next to me smiled and indicated that I should write down what Madame said. I felt grateful for her friendliness, although she seemed a bit odd. Stains spotted her smock, which had holes in it. Where almost all the other girls looked shiny and coiffed, her hands and face were dirty and her dark hair uncombed. Still, she didn't laugh at me. Watching my classmates out of the corner of my eye, I tried to copy their actions. I dipped the pen in the inkwell and applied it to the paper, struggling to print out letters that might be related to the words coming out of *Madame la Maîtresse*'s mouth.

I pressed too hard, tore the page, splattered ink and snapped the nib. Unsure what to do, I sat still, watching enviously as the other girls not only dipped without splotching, but actually wrote out the words, longhand. I did not even know how to read longhand, let alone write it. And these girls were only entering Grade Two?

At last the exercise, which I later learned was called a *dictée* (Dictation), ended. *Madame la Maîtresse* moved up and down the aisles gathering up the exercise books (*cahiers*). When she reached me, she seized my blotched notebook and shouted at me. I swallowed back tears. I would NOT cry in front of these hostile strangers. I explained that I didn't know how to use a nib pen and didn't understand the words she'd been saying, let alone how to spell them, since I now realized this was some sort of spelling test. Titters ran through the class as the girls watched the scene, whispering to each other and rolling their eyes.

After shouting at me some more, Madame collected the rest of the books. Then she returned to me with a pencil.

I seized it with relief. She watched as I printed my name. I wanted her to know I did at least know how to print.

"*Mon dieu!*" she muttered. Then she jabbed her finger at the paper and said, "*Histoire.*"

I'd got the idea, so I printed out *e-a-s-t-w-a-r-r-e.*

She slapped her forehead. "*Imbecile!*"

I dutifully wrote *a-m-b-a-y-s-e-e-l.*

She grabbed my notebook, marked it with an enormous X and returned to her desk. The girls fell about in amusement; she shouted them into silence.

The morning dragged on. When a bell rang and the other girls raced out into the courtyard, I wanted to put my head down and sob. But the girl next to me, whose name appeared to be Baggasin, smiled and spoke gently to me. She rose and encouraged me with gestures to follow her outside, wiping her runny nose on her sleeve. I followed, grateful for her kindness. We crouched against the wall and she talked to me and drew a picture in the dirt. None of the other girls came near us, but I could feel their disapproving eyes.

The class resumed. I couldn't do anything right. In fact, I couldn't do anything at all, since I had no idea what was being demanded of me. By some small miracle, the first day ended at lunchtime. I raced out of the school and ran smack into my mother, who'd come to fetch me. Her smile dissolved when she saw my face. I marched home in silence, fighting tears, refusing to answer her cheerful questions. Once the door to *6 rue Nicolet* had crashed shut behind us, I exploded.

"How could you send me to that awful place?" I howled. "They're all idiots. They don't speak any English. The teacher is mean. She shouted at me! I broke my pen. They all know how to write, and they have pretty smocks and the only girl who was nice to me at all has snot on her sleeve! I'm NOT going back. Ever."

"Oh sweetie." My mother stroked my hair. "It'll get better. It's just all new—"

"No. It will *not* get better. I hate them. Why did we have to come here? I want to go home," I wailed, dissolving in tears.

That afternoon, while I sobbed on the couch, my mother marched off to the school to speak to the teacher. I wondered if *Madame la Maîtresse* would treat her with the kind of scorn she'd showered on me, but I doubted it. My mother, though small, could be fierce. My father hugged me and persuaded me to go out for a pastry. Despite my distress, I chomped it down. My mother returned, her face tight, to tell me she had explained the situation and *Madame la Maîtresse* had promised to be more patient and understanding. I didn't believe it. I wondered if she had spoken to the teacher at all.

When Frances and Neil came home, I could tell they'd had better days. The teachers at their *lycée* sounded pretty tough. Stupid French people, I thought. They're just plain mean. But at least Frances and Neil had classmates who spoke English. My parents obviously cared more about my siblings' comfort than mine.

That evening, everyone tried to console me. Worry had replaced the joy in my parents' faces. Worry and guilt, I hoped. Still, they held firm, telling me it would get better. My mother would buy me a smock right away. I would learn French. In fact, the best way to learn was by immersion (whatever that meant). In no time, I would be speaking French better than anyone in the family. Lies. They had no idea what it was like in that classroom. They didn't understand.

I cried myself to sleep and awoke the next morning determined to resist. At breakfast, I screamed my refusal again. After a heated argument, my parents drove me to school. When we arrived, school had obviously begun. No children streamed through the huge doorway or frolicked in the courtyard beyond.

"I can't go in now," I whimpered, hoping they would see the wisdom of this and allow me to stay home, even just for one day.

"Yes, you can." My mother's voice had an edge to it. "You're only a few minutes late. Run on in."

I slammed out of the car and ran into the courtyard. As soon as I turned the corner out of sight, I stopped. Silence enclosed the courtyard, punctuated by the distant voices of the *maîtresses*. I could not enter the classroom now and face all those hostile French eyes. I took a few deep breaths. No one knew I was here. My parents were off to explore Paris for the day. Hugging the walls, I edged around the courtyard to the back entrance. Still no one emerged to catch me. I crashed through the door and out onto an unfamiliar street.

Brakes squealed. My parents' car pulled over. Caught. I stood stony-faced. Apparently, they'd been talking while I hid in the courtyard. Something had changed.

My mother stifled a smile. "I told you," she murmured to my dad.

"Meg," said my father. "We know you aren't very happy at this school."

I nodded, my eyes filling. They *did* understand.

"But you also know you have to go to school."

Again, I nodded. *Of course* I knew that. "Could I go to the *lycée* with Frances and Neil?"

"You're not old enough. It's high school," my mother said.

"But—" I felt certain I'd heard some mention of an American school for younger students beside the *lycée*.

"Honey, it would be too far for you to travel. Besides, this is the best way to learn French—"

"I don't want to learn French! I *can't* go in there now. They'd all laugh at me. It's too late!"

"Shh, it's okay." My mother wrapped her arms around me.

"How about we make a deal," said my father. "You can stay home today if you promise to go back tomorrow and stick with it."

This is the kind of crafty deal parents make with children. Of course, I didn't want to go back, ever, but above all I couldn't bear the thought of arriving late. "Okay," I said, sounding as pathetic as I could.

That afternoon my mother took me to the *Prisunic*, a department store that sold clothes. She had learned, in her conversation with *la maîtresse*, that the little smocks were called *tabliers*, which means aprons, although these did not resemble the kinds of aprons my mother wore, because they had sleeves and buttoned up the front. We made our way along the aisles to the *tabliers de l'école*. My mother refused to buy the nicest *tablier* because it was too expensive. In the end, we compromised on a pale blue one, not as pretty as some, but so much better than the ratty grey one I'd worn the day before.

"Will it do?" my mother asked.

I nodded. It would do. At least tomorrow I would arrive properly dressed. And on time.

The next day I encountered a new challenge at school. I needed to use the toilet. I knew there must be a toilet and had seen girls asking questions before leaving the room. I just didn't know what question to ask or where to go. I held on until recess, crossing my legs. As we streamed out into the courtyard, I saw a couple of the girls head down the corridor and disappear through a door.

I tapped Baggasin on the arm and pointed after the girls. To my relief, she nodded, smiling in her vacant way, took me by the hand, and led me along the corridor. I shrank when *Madame la Maîtresse* came out of the classroom and barked a question at us. Baggasin's response seemed to satisfy her and she re-entered the classroom. As we reached the door, the two girls emerged, laughing, and stepped aside to avoid us, as though we were contaminated.

Baggasin pushed open the door. The room reeked of urine, so I knew we'd come to the right place. Baggasin indicated a stall and disappeared into the one beside it. I pushed open the wooden door to find a hole in the floor with a metal footpad on either side. I backed out. Obviously, the toilet had been removed or maybe this was intended for boys who could stand up and pee. I waited, not too patiently, until Baggasin emerged from her stall. She gave me a funny look and I gestured to indicate the stall was out of order. She frowned, then opened the door to the stall she'd just vacated. It was exactly the same.

I could not believe she thought I would use that stinking hole as a toilet. Some joke. No human being, surely, would do so! My feelings must have shown on my face, for Baggasin nodded encouragingly and guided me in, closing the door to give me some privacy. The stench made me gag. Holding my breath, I tiptoed through the vile splatters, stepped gingerly onto the footpads, crouched down and peed as quickly as

I could, hoping I wasn't splashing my shoes and socks. A glance around from my scrunched position revealed another problem: no toilet paper. I had peed in the woods on camping trips in Canada. I knew how to drip-dry, but in a school? Unbelievable! I finished my business and bolted out past Baggasin, into the courtyard, feeling filthy. The French were barbarians, even if they could write with nib pens. Pursing my lips, I decided I would never again use the toilets at school. I ignored Baggasin for the rest of the day, as though it were all her fault.

Madame la Maîtresse stopped calling me *imbecile* and shouting at me. I continued to submit horrible *dictées*, without a word spelled right. I made no attempt to speak French. It would have been too embarrassing. Better to stay silent and let my peers reach whatever conclusions they liked about *la petite Anglaise*, as they called me, than risk their scorn with faulty attempts to speak their language.

Sometimes I spoke a very little to Baggasin, once I'd recovered from the toilet episode. She continued to be friendly, although I gradually realized she was an outcast, not just because of her filthy appearance, but because she was not very smart. Baggasin was her last name and it was something of an insult to address her this way. All the other girls were called by their first names. They called me Margaret, pronounced as three distinct syllables: Mar-gar-ette. No one could pronounce Meg and I used my full name to keep things simple, even though I disliked it. My mother's name was Margaret and I had always been Meg. Still, it served as a sort of shield. It wasn't me being insulted and scorned at school; it was Mar-gar-ette.

4

The Challenges of French Food

To my relief, I discovered I could hold my own in two subjects at school: arithmetic and gym. Apart from the little slash across the seven, the numbers and symbols in arithmetic were the same as in Canada, and I was quite adept at adding and subtracting. My prowess in gym astonished me. I'd never been athletic. Now I found myself at an advantage because of my relative height, since we did a lot of jumping and running. I continued to perform miserably in other subjects, but I did pretty well in these two. This success boosted my self-esteem.

Fearing the mockery of my classmates—not to mention *Madame la Maîtresse*—I tried not to draw attention to myself. I arrived at school just as the bell rang. At lunchtime and at the end of the day, I raced out of the courtyard and home without a backward glance. At recess, which was thankfully brief, Baggasin kept me company.

My parents now let me walk to and from school on my own. At lunch, my mother prepared my favourite foods:

macaroni and cheese made from scratch, baguettes with thin sliced ham, chicken soups, and fresh fruit. The midday break gave me strength to endure the afternoon.

Then one day *Madame la Maîtresse* handed out little slips of paper to take home. She gabbled at us fiercely and I heard oohs and aahs from the other girls: some kind of big news. When I got home and presented the note to my mother, she peered at it for some time and tut-tutted.

"What is it?" I asked. The girls had seemed quite excited. I thought it might be a class trip, an intriguing and worrisome idea.

My mother rubbed her nose and gave a little sigh. "It says that the school is … They are going to be doing some renovations to the building, and for a few months you will have to go to another school."

"Why me?"

She stared at me blankly, then laughed. "Not just you. All the students. It says you will walk to the other school together in the morning and back again in the afternoon."

I didn't like the sound of this.

She bit her lip. "And you won't be able to come home for lunch. It's too far away."

Oh great. I'd have to walk for hours with the girls making fun of me and I wouldn't even get a break for lunch.

"But they'll serve lunch at the new school and we can sign you up for the program. Imagine. Hot lunch every day—and the French cook so well."

"Yeah. Great."

Monday morning, *Madame la Maîtresse* called us to order in the courtyard and shepherded us into a long line, three abreast. My classmates raced to walk with their closest friends, fighting for the honour of accompanying the most popular girls. Needless to say, no one rushed to my side. Baggasin and I walked at the back with some unfortunate who'd been too late to nab better companions. We left through the main door, holding hands in our threesomes, and walked down the main boulevard, across a busy intersection, and along another eight blocks of side streets. Most of the girls regarded this as a lark; they giggled and chatted merrily. I marched along in silence.

The new school seemed much like the old, with a similar enclosed courtyard where we spent recess and lunch hour. My mother had sent me back to school with a little note and a few francs to cover the cost of lunch. When the noon bell rang, some of the girls left the premises. I assume they had kind, thoughtful parents who took them home for lunch. The rest of us filed into a long room with tables. A few girls had brought lunch and proceeded to open their little cloth bags and baskets.

The rest of us lined up to receive trays. An overweight woman slapped food onto each tray: a mug of water, a chunk of bread, a fat slab of sausage, a bowl of greasy soup, and a smaller bowl of something smooth and white—dessert, I assumed. I managed to gnaw down the bread and sausage and most of the thin soup. Full, I decided to ignore the white stuff. The lumpy woman in charge pointed at it, frowned and said something sharp to me. I took a small spoonful and almost threw up. The thick pasty substance tasted sour, as in going-bad curdled sour. I pushed it away. The lumpy one indicated I should finish it. I shook my head, aware that I had the full attention of the other girls, who happily spooned the disgusting stuff into their mouths. Lumpy crossed her arms and spoke sternly to me. I glared at her. Then she clapped her hands and the girls all rose and pelted out into the sunshine. I jumped up too. She pushed me back onto the bench and shoved the goo in front of me.

I indignantly explained that I was not going to eat it. Who forced children to eat dessert? The thought gave me pause. It didn't taste like dessert. Maybe it wasn't. Maybe it was supposed to be healthy. Sweat broke out on my forehead. She shouted at me, grabbed the spoon, and forced some of it into my mouth. I swallowed, feeling bile rise in my throat. Then I burst into tears.

Despite Lumpy's rage, I did not finish the stuff, which I later discovered was yoghurt. I had never encountered it before and years passed before I found it palatable; the mere scent brought this memory rushing back, stimulating my gag reflex.

By the time I reached home, having endured the humiliation of being the last person in line for the second time, I was inconsolable.

"I can't stand it," I wailed.

My mother looked wan, as so often when she dealt with me these days.

"They *forced* me to eat this horrible sour guck. I almost threw up. I never, never want to eat there again."

My mother heard me out. Later she muttered to my father, "It's the most ridiculous thing I ever heard. It never crossed my mind that they'd force her to eat. I mean, we paid for it. Not like it was a handout or anything. Honestly."

The next day, I took a packed lunch, not in one of the clever little satchels the other girls had, but in a plain paper bag. I didn't care. At least my mother wouldn't try to poison me.

Given my almost non-existent appetite, eating was an ongoing challenge. In 1963, there was no fresh milk in France, so my mother bought preserved milk in triangular boxes. It had a faintly rotten chemical taste. I could barely stomach it. This frazzled my mother, who had a hearty North American respect for milk and could not imagine a child growing up without it, especially a sickly child like me. We fought about milk on a daily basis. I held my nose to drink it. My mother tried to create something like chocolate milk, without the advantage of Quik; the mixture ended up being unpleasantly granular but tasted a bit better.

My parents rolled their eyes at the French custom of allowing their children to drink watered-down wine in restaurants. "Probably at home, too," my mother muttered. I'd never tasted wine and would have hated it, but sometimes I thought anything would be better than the putrid milk.

The entire family pined for peanut butter and maple syrup, but we delighted in fresh, hot baguettes every morning. I got to know the lady in the *boulangerie*, who thought me "*très mignonne*", which sounded better than "cute". Since I rose earlier than anyone else, it became my job to trot down our tiny *rue* in the dark and join the line at the *boulangerie*. The lady was so kind to me that I risked my first French words with her. I listened to all the other people asking for "*une baguette*" or "*deux baguettes, s'il vous plaît.*" I knew my numbers in French, so I managed to ask the question correctly. The lady beamed at me, said, "*Bien sure, ma petite*," and handed over the long warm loaves. Grinning at my small triumph and intoxicated by the fresh bread smell, I scurried home for breakfast.

The *pâtisseries* in Paris emitted the most delicious aromas and I would linger at their windows, gazing at the *éclairs* and *tartes* and hundred other treats just beyond the glass. Yet, when I persuaded my mother or father to indulge me, I was often disappointed. At home, I'd been passionate about chocolate éclairs, because of their whipped cream fillings. In Paris, they often filled the éclairs with custard, which had the consistency of yoghurt. More appallingly, many pastries and cakes were laced with liquor, which I hated.

Many familiar, comforting foods, like Kraft Dinner, could not be purchased in France. Given this dismal fact and my parents' enthusiasm for new flavours, eventually I had to experiment, although I did so very carefully, always suspicious that something yoghurt-like might be concealed in the new food. I enjoyed many offerings from the *charcuterie*: vinaigrette carrots and especially *remoulade*, a salad of thinly slivered celeriac and mayonnaise. And the Suchard chocolate bars were divine. I'd have lived on them except some people, of the parental variety, thought too much chocolate might not be good for a growing girl.

One day my mother returned from the market with a peculiar new vegetable, an artichoke. She proudly plopped several of the green sharp-leaved bulbs on the table. They looked a most unlikely foodstuff. My mother hacked off the spiked ends of the leaves with some difficulty and then boiled them for a long time. I narrowed my eyes as she placed one of these now grayish spheres on a plate before me.

"They look awful." I prodded the artichoke with a fork. It felt hard and tough, even after all that boiling.

"It's a rarity," she said, ladling melted butter and lemon juice into little bowls. "You can get artichokes in California, but I've never seen them as big as these. They're Globe artichokes, supposed to be delicious."

Big did not strike me as good; it just meant I'd have to struggle through more of it.

"You don't use a fork," my mother explained. "You tear off one leaf at a time." She showed me. "Dip the bottom end of it into the lemon butter and pull off the soft part with your teeth." She did so, swallowed and smiled. "Then you discard the rest of the leaf. It's inedible."

I thought the whole thing looked inedible, but the lemon butter smelled sweet. Everyone else tore at the leaves with their teeth and made moaning noises.

"Just try a bite," wheedled my mother.

To appease her, I torn off a large leaf, dipped the thick end into the butter, and pulled the little mound of grey pulp off with my teeth. An extraordinary flavour filled my mouth, delicate, delectable, unearthly. I fell in love. Not just with the sublime taste, but the entire ritual. Tearing, dipping, drawing the flesh into my mouth. As we progressed leaf by leaf, the artichoke shrank, the leaves grew smaller and thinner, and then the heart appeared.

"Now you have to scrape away the choke," said my mother, taking her knife and gently cutting out the coarse fur in the centre of the artichoke. "Then you eat the heart itself."

I hastened to follow her example, clearing away the choke, slicing the big chunk of heart into pieces and dipping them in the lemon butter. I leaned back in a state of bliss, certain I could eat artichokes at every meal for the rest of my life.

5

Courtyard Neighbours

With the exception of gym and arithmetic, school continued to be miserable. The French school system, as my parents agreed in hushed tones when they thought I couldn't hear, was a great deal more advanced than our Canadian one. Not only did all my perfectly appointed classmates write beautiful ink script, they knew history, geography, and science at levels well beyond my own. Not to mention the convolutions of French grammar and spelling. I continued to get large red Xs on my *dictées*. We had to memorize passages called *resumés* (summaries) and recite them aloud under *Madame la Maîtresse*'s fierce glare. My hands grew clammy every time I had to stand before the class of highly amused girls.

No doubt my unhappiness worried my parents, but what could they do? Having taken the fatal step of placing me in that wretched school, they had to hold firm to their belief that it would all work out and this would ultimately be a Good Experience. Despite putting such emphasis on education, they couldn't help me with my schoolwork. They took me to the *librarie*, which in typical French fashion was not a library at all, but a shop that sold writing materials. There my mother purchased me a nib pen and inkpot, some *cahiers*, and one of the little slates on which we did our sums. The entire family tried to work out pronunciations to help me memorize and recite the *resumés*. But I knew I'd never master this infuriating language. I didn't even want to.

Help came from an unlikely quarter. The door of our house opened onto the narrow sidewalk of *rue Nicolet* and had the number 6 above it. Right next to it stood another door, marked 6 *bis*. That door did not open into another house but into a low-ceilinged corridor that led to the stinky courtyard behind our house. Shoddy-looking people came and went through the 6 *bis* door. Our housekeeper also used that entranceway, as the little half door into our laundry room opened off the corridor.

The courtyard both frightened and fascinated me. I'd peer down from the safety of the Room With A View. Several doors opened onto the courtyard and people scurried in and out of them. I imagined the occupants of these dwellings to be not only poor but possibly criminal. Perhaps the tall man in the tattered coat kidnapped eight-year-old girls. The old lady wearing a black kerchief might be an evil gypsy and the skinny man with glasses could be a thief. They all struck me as furtive and potentially dangerous, living behind the scenes. When they passed me to enter the 6 *bis* door, I pretended not to see them.

One day as my mother and I returned from shopping, we encountered a woman in her forties with coiffed blonde hair at that doorway. A tall pale young woman accompanied her. Although they appeared quite normal, I quickly looked away.

Ignoring my discomfort, the older woman began to jabber away in French, saying things like, "*Elle est si mignonne, la petite*" in a high bright voice. Beaming, she reached out to pinch my chin. She didn't sound or look like a witch, but I'd read *Hansel and Gretel*.

My mother, speaking with painful slowness, explained that we didn't really speak French.

The young woman spoke. "You arrrre Engleesh?"

My mother and I exchanged an astonished glance.

"Yes," said my mother. "You speak English?"

The young woman nodded. "A leetle bit. I am studying at the univairsitay."

My mother gave a small gasp.

In short order, we learned that Madame Wax and her daughter Marie-Laurence occupied a second floor flat off the courtyard. They had odd names, certainly; Wax sounded more English than French, and Marie-Laurence was a confusing combination of girl's and boy's names, not to mention a mouthful. But they did not seem like criminals or ne'er-do-wells. No Baggasins, for sure. And Madame Wax couldn't take her eyes off me. After the continual rejection at school, I found her attention rather pleasing. I smiled up at her; she batted her eyes at me, beaming.

Almost immediately, Madame Wax invited the whole family over to visit. Or rather, Marie-Laurence conveyed her mother's message to us in English. Madame Wax looked giddy with excitement; Marie-Laurence was calm, almost aloof.

"Do you think it's a good idea?" my father asked, when my mother told him.

My mother shrugged. "Who knows? It can't do any harm. She seemed friendly enough, and the daughter does speak English."

I think my mother liked the idea of befriending neighbours, even if they lived "off the courtyard." Mostly she loved the thought of being able to converse in English with a Parisian.

At the appointed hour, the five of us trooped along the dim corridor and across the courtyard. I glanced about, but no tramps lurked in the corners. Curtains covered the lit windows. Shapes moved about within, but none seemed threatening. We climbed a narrow set of stairs. As my mother reached out to tap on the door, it flew open and Madame Wax burst out, or at least she would have had there been room. She'd clearly prepared for the visit; she wore a bright flowered dress, lipstick, and perfume. She ushered us in, giggling, and swept me into a hug, crushing me to her. Then she held me back at arm's length and proceeded to plant a kiss on each of my cheeks. While more intimate than I liked, this was a familiar Parisian form of greeting. Whenever people met, they smacked each other's cheeks. It struck me as odd that they could be so familiar, when they spoke so formally. Men were always referred to as *Monsieur* and women as *Madame*. Adults addressed even young girls like me as *Madamoiselle*; I rather liked that.

We crowded into a tiny overheated apartment. It contained only a bedroom that they shared, a living room jammed with mismatched furniture, and a kitchen in which you could not turn around. Our modest little house seemed like a palace in comparison. In the living room, we squished ourselves into the furniture. Madame Wax chattered away merrily.

Marie-Laurence calmly translated the obvious. "My mother is verrry glad to see you. She theenks your leettle daughter is charming."

I grinned. Madame pulled me onto her lap as though I were a large doll and proceeded to offer me sweets. I hesitated, remembering the witch and her candy house. Madame winked at me. I plopped a candy into my mouth; it tasted fine. Marie-Laurence poured wine into heavy glasses. She asked my mother, "Would the leettle one like water with her wine?"

My mother almost choked. "Ah, actually Meg doesn't drink wine."

Marie-Laurence shrugged. "In France, children often drink wine, but with water, of courrrse."

My mother said sweetly, "In Canada children do not drink."

Marie-Laurence conveyed this information to Madame Wax, who responded with a trill of laughter. Mostly, however, she ignored the adults and focused on me. I began to feel overwhelmed by her cloying attention, not to mention the sweets.

Marie-Laurence did her best to carry on the stilted conversation, mostly translating for her mother. My father, red-faced from the heat, looked bored. Frances and Neil squirmed on the sofa.

They wanted to know all about us: where we'd come from, how long we'd been here, where I went to school, what I liked about Paris, what I thought of my teacher.

"Meg is having some trouble because she does not speak French," said my mother.

Madame Wax let forth an animated tirade, gesticulating in astonishment. The French, I knew from bitter experience, had trouble imagining that anyone could survive without speaking their language. At length, however, Marie-Laurence seemed to persuade her that such a situation could indeed exist. Madame took a deep breath, muttered something to Marie-Laurence and prodded her.

"I would be happy to help Meeg with her schoolwork, if you would like," said Marie-Laurence. I heard no hint of enthusiasm.

"Call me Mar-gar-ette," I said quickly. Meeg. Really.

Madame Wax giggled and chanted, "Margarette, Margarette, Margarette."

My mother gave me a *don't be rude* look. "That is very kind of you," she said to Marie-Laurence. "But are you sure? We would not want to impose."

"It would be my pleasure," said Marie-Laurence unconvincingly. "It would help me with my English."

My mother fell all over herself with gratitude. "That would be most helpful. She is having such a hard time at school. The other children are impatient with her and she struggles so."

I tried to look as though it didn't matter to me in the slightest. When Marie-Laurence translated, Madame Wax looked like she might burst into tears. She hugged me tightly, murmuring reassurances, and then gabbled in angry tones, waving her arms.

"My mother theenks it is ...disgraceful that the children are not kind to Margarette," said Marie-Laurence.

I smiled at Madame; she kissed me again.

We escaped as soon as we could, despite Madame's objections and offers of more wine, more pastries, more candy.

My father thought Madame Wax unbearably childish.

"Yes, she's very odd," said my mother. "Marie-Laurence seems the more mature of the two." We'd learned that Marie-Laurence was twenty-two years old.

"Why on earth is she still living at home?" asked my father. "In that tiny little place where she can never escape her mother."

In our world, children left home as soon as they went to university. It was part of growing up. Neil could hardly wait to get away.

"Poor Marie-Laurence," sighed my mother. "They're probably too poor for her to live on her own."

"But she's twenty-two," said Frances. "No one lives with their parents when they're twenty-two! How awful for her!"

"Maybe she stays with Madame Wax because the poor woman couldn't manage on her own," said my mother.

I felt a little nervous about Marie-Laurence helping me with homework. Could a grown-up woman really want to spend time teaching an eight-year-old? My parents brushed off my concerns, pleased that someone might be able to help me.

At my first solo visit, Madame Wax fussed over me, but eventually withdrew to a corner and let Marie-Laurence take charge. While never warm, Marie-Laurence proved a patient teacher. She showed me how to dip my pen in the ink and hold it until it stopped dripping, how to apply the pen to paper without splattering the ink or tearing the page and how to form those perfect letters. She explained the assignments, translated, helped me with pronunciation, and drilled me on my *resumés*.

It did not take long for Marie-Laurence to get me on track. I'd already begun to absorb some words and had figured out, through observation, most of what I was supposed to do. Nonetheless, it boosted my confidence to know I had a supporter, someone in my camp who could explain the inexplicable. As I began to learn French, a ray of light pierced my gloom; I might someday be able to speak this cursèd language after all!

6

Jeudi

Although at first it struck me as peculiar, I came to like the school schedule in France. Rather than having weekends free, we had Thursday and Sunday off, Thursday being *jeudi,* or Play Day as I liked to think of it. Parisians devoted Thursdays to children. Parents took the day off work, or, in my case, away from exploring Paris or writing (my father was working on a book). All over Paris events for children took place, and it became a highlight of the week to spend the day with one or both of my parents, visiting unusual places and taking part in these child-oriented activities. My siblings, at an American school, had weekends off, so for one day a week I got my parents all to myself. I suspect they went out of their way to make Thursdays special, to compensate for the hard time I was having at school.

In fine weather, even I fell under the city's charm. My parents knew better than to take me to art galleries or cathedrals, but I loved accompanying my mother to the market, eyeing all the fresh produce, especially the artichokes, and watching her haggle with large French women. My parents bought me ice cream at the *glaceries*. We rode the hot smelly metro and emerged onto wide boulevards. My mother located an English library and I checked out books of adventure stories. We promenaded along the Seine, examining the ancient maps, books, and posters in the stalls on the left bank. We scaled the incredibly long staircase to the top of Montmartre and gazed out over all of Paris. The Eiffel Tower reminded me of the castle spire on the Walt Disney credits: enchanted, delicate, unique.

Through the autumn, we wandered the streets and parks of Paris in golden sunlight, the tall trees plunging us into dappled shadow. Above all, I loved to visit the Tuileries—*les jardins des Tuileries*—the formal French gardens that extend a great distance from the front of the Louvre. I preferred to think of the Louvre as the famous palace where a bunch of King Louies lived, rather than the immense, exhausting museum through which I'd been dragged early in our stay. Why people fell all over themselves looking at some dowdy dark-haired woman who didn't know how to smile properly or the massive statue of a woman without arms, I could not figure. But the idea of kings and queens being beheaded thrilled me.

Children filled the Tuileries on *jeudi*, picnicking with their parents, riding the carousel, and giggling at puppet shows. These lively performances took place in elaborately decorated little booths. Some resembled Punch and Judy shows but others were heroic tales, and I liked these best. The puppets, in their bright outfits, bobbing up and down, made me laugh and shriek, even if I couldn't understand the words they spoke. I dragged my parents back to the Tuileries over and over again. I don't think they minded. The park featured a café and was beautifully groomed and quiet, apart from the laughter of children.

During these days, I learned about my parents' experiences in Paris. Often, they would spend the whole day walking. Other times they plunged into excited explorations of Parisian cuisine. Both my parents were thrilled to be living in the culinary capitol of the world. They wanted to taste everything, no matter how peculiar. They dined on *escargots* (snails!), scallops, strange mushrooms, revolting-smelling cheeses, tripe, and any number of other repulsive things. Sometimes my mother experimented with cooking such fare, but mostly they saved up their money and went to restaurants.

As the year progressed, they began to see themselves as connoisseurs, although some Parisian habits, like drinking generous quantities of wine at midday, astounded them.

"Could you believe that man?" my father exclaimed as we lounged in the Tuileries one afternoon. "A businessman— and he drank an entire bottle of wine, by himself, at lunch! I don't know how he could possibly work after that."

Nonetheless, they had to experiment. A few days later, they split a bottle of wine at lunchtime, and reeled home from the restaurant, jolly but sure they could never manage this on a daily basis. The sense of adventure in their voices made me smile.

Another time, they splurged and went to a Three Star Restaurant. I wondered if they were going to eat starfish, but figured, more likely, the restaurant had stars on the ceiling or something. They couldn't stop talking about it: the linen tablecloths and polished silverware, the black-clad waiters with their silver trays, the sauces, the presentations, the air of refinement and, above all, the wonderful food.

During their exquisite meal, a group of loud American businessmen sat at a nearby table, swilling martinis. When the waiter took their order, according to my dad, the Americans seemed to be sloshed. But the waiter treated them with immense respect.

"Then they ordered a 60-year-old bottle of Chateau Margaux—a very old, rare wine," he explained in hushed tones. "It cost over 1000 francs. They probably just ordered it because it was the most expensive wine on the menu."

This sounded like nonsense to me. A bottle of wine worth that much money?

My parents watched in fascination as the waiter returned, cradling the bottle, and placed it gingerly on the sideboard. The drunk Americans paid no attention. The waiter opened the bottle. He raised it to his nose. His face lit up. He turned slightly away from the table and filled a glass. He tasted it, sighed, then drank the whole glass.

"Then he carried the wine to the table, poured a small tasting glass and waited. The American knocked it back and nodded. The waiter filled their glasses, as polite as ever. He'd just drunk probably 200 francs worth of their wine and they didn't even notice!" said my father. "It just goes to show how Parisians value fine wine. No waiter worth his salt could stand to see ignorant slobs waste a Chateau Margaux."

Their understanding of this important fact clearly made them feel they had the pulse of Parisian life.

Gradually we all began to feel we belonged in Paris. Shopkeepers recognized us. Madame Wax and Marie-Laurence greeted us cheerily when we passed them on the street. We knew our way around the neighbourhood. My parents nodded to the proprietors of their favourite cafés and bistros. My siblings had mastered the complex metro route to their school and made some friends.

Even I made friends. Not at school, where the girls still ignored me, but on the street.

In Montreal West, we had a front porch with a small lawn and a big backyard with flowerbeds. All my life I'd played with neighbouring children. Indeed, I'd pretty much called the shots, as two younger children lived on one side of our house and a Russian girl lived on the other. (When I first met her, she couldn't speak a word of English and I suspect I treated her almost as badly as my French schoolmates were now treating me.) We played outside all the time, on the sidewalks and in each other's backyards.

In Paris, we had no lawns or gardens. Our front door opened directly onto a tiny sidewalk on a very narrow street, along which only a single car could drive. When cars encountered each other, the drivers honked their horns and shouted until one or the other eventually backed up to allow passage. Worst of all, nobody played outside. Anywhere. I saw children in the parks and the cafés and at school, but never playing on the streets.

Then one day I spotted two brown-skinned children sitting on the curb of *rue Nicolet*, playing with sticks. The boy looked to be about my age, the girl a couple of years younger. My desire for playmates quickly overcame my shyness. These children were not in my class, so there seemed little danger that they would know of my incompetence. I inched toward them, at first watching from the doorstep, then moving a little closer, always pretending disinterest. They saw me, but neither turned away nor welcomed me. We watched each other out of the corners of our eyes. For about twenty minutes. Then I moved closer, the little girl smiled and I joined their game.

Patrick (pa-**treek**) and Josée lived a few houses further up *rue Nicolet* and spent a lot of time outside. Unlike my school companions, they didn't seem bothered by my lack of French, nor did they mock me when I tried to communicate. Josée smiled and nodded and they made a game of figuring out what I wanted to say. No judgment or concern. We became a trio, playing hopscotch, drawing in the dirt with sticks, chasing each other around, and squealing in glee.

My mother was a little concerned about both the amount of time I spent on the street and the children themselves. Who were their parents? Why were they outside so much? I couldn't have cared less, but she clearly disapproved. They didn't seem like well brought-up children. Their worn clothes did not look terribly clean; dirt smudged their hands. I didn't look much better after playing in the gutter. I doubt she worried about them being of mixed race, but likely that put them low on the social ladder in Paris at the time.

In the end, she allowed me to play with them and even suggested I bring them inside, although she must have been terrified about Louie's furniture. They refused to come in; their parents would not allow them to enter strangers' homes. My mother pursed her lips at this, perhaps insulted that her generous invitation had been refused. Had I not been so lonely, she'd probably have put her foot down and told me I couldn't play with them at all, but like all of us, she'd adjusted to the oddities of life in Paris and was not about to deny me some pleasure.

Now I rushed home from school to play. My French improved rapidly, with Patrick and Josée encouraging me, correcting my pronunciation, and applauding my improvement like proud parents. Between my street urchin friends and beautiful *jeudis* with my parents, life in Paris became bearable.

7

Ooh La La!

I still did not speak at school, beyond giving painful recitations of the assigned *resumés*. Insulted and hurt by the scornful attitude of both my classmates and *Madame la Maîtresse*, I did as I always did in such circumstances: I withdrew. I refused to make a fool of myself by speaking incorrectly, so I did not speak at all. Although everyone concluded I was an idiot, incapable of speech and maybe even thought, they mocked me less. I think they stopped seeing me. My silence made me almost invisible.

Relieved, I set out to master the language without uttering a word. I listened and watched and before long, I could follow their conversations fairly well. I also contemplated revenge. I would show them. One day, when I felt confident that I could speak perfectly, I would open my mouth and dazzle them all. They would be astonished and feel very, very badly about the way they'd treated me. In fact, they would be the ones to look stupid, for assuming I had no brains just because I wasn't speaking. These thoughts comforted me.

In truth, I wanted them to like me. I yearned to be friends with these pretty, bubbly girls. I studied them, hoping to discover a way into their good graces, and soon realized that the most popular girls were also the students who received the best marks. How could I possibly attract their interest, given my dismal academic record?

Madame la Maîtresse's strict, condescending manner never wavered. She did not smile. Nor did she applaud even the best students, the ones who recited their *resumés* flawlessly and wrote perfect *dictées*. The names of the highest achievers did not appear on the chalkboard at the front, nor did anyone receive gold stars in their *cahiers*. At first, I thought the French system cold and mean-spirited. In Montreal West, pictures and colourful diagrams hung on classroom walls. Not so in Paris. Madame wrote on the board. We wrote in our *cahiers* or on our little slates, at desks perfectly regimented into rows. We even walked to school in perfect lines.

The French rewards for academic achievement were similarly regimented. For each successful assignment completed, one received a small ticket with the words *Bon Point* printed on it. I watched *Madame la Maîtresse* handing these out over the first few weeks. It seemed a silly reward to me, a stupid little ticket. Not nearly as nice as a shiny gold star. But by the time I received my first *Bon Point*, for arithmetic, I knew these tickets had value.

If you amassed ten *Bon Points* in your desk, you could exchange them for a *Petite Image*, a little picture about the size of a playing card. And ten *Petite Images* could be traded in for the ultimate award: a *Grande Image*, a larger glossier postcard-sized picture. Illustrations of all sorts adorned both sizes of *image:* landscapes and castles and bridges, heroic figures, clowns, princesses, acrobats, and animals of every kind, vividly coloured. I watched enviously as the brighter girls gathered more and more of these infinitely desirable cards. With my meagre store of *Bon Points,* it seemed unlikely I would ever receive a *Petite Image,* let alone a *Grande* one. Yet clearly, I had to make this my ambition, if I were to make friends with the right girls.

The connection between academic success and popularity surprised me. In Montreal West, only wealth seemed to make any difference, and even that in a minimal way, perhaps because we were all essentially middle class. In 1963, no poor people lived in Montreal West, no street urchins or dirty children, no foreigners or people of colour.

In Paris, financial and class issues may have had some bearing, but none that I noticed, except in the case of Baggasin. The most popular girls were the ones who did best at school, perhaps simply because they were able to amass the *Grandes Images.* Those less capable fluttered around these mini scholars, seeking their favours, desperate to gaze upon those elusive *Images.* I was no different. I too craned to catch a glimpse of the *Grandes Images* as the smarter girls collected them, and I longed to receive one as much because it would impress my peers as for the delight of possessing the picture.

I wanted these girls to recognize that I could excel at school too. I yearned for attention from three particular girls. Solange, with her dark blonde hair, brown eyes, and mischievous grin was clearly the top student, *la première dans la classe.* She received the very first *Grande Image* of the year. The girls rushed to her side at the break and she proudly showed them the picture she'd had the honour to select from the box Madame extended to her. "*Ooh la la!*" her admirers gasped. I struggled to comprehend this common phrase. Mostly the girls (and even women at the market) used it to express delight, but sometimes, when they rolled their eyes, it had sarcastic overtones. In this instance, it clearly meant "Wow! Fantastic!" Try as I might (without, of course, seeming to) I could not get a glimpse of her *Image.*

Solange never even glanced in my direction and I hung back from the eager crowd who constantly surrounded her. Still, I dreamt that someday, perhaps when I received such an honour, she would favour me with her smile.

Danielle rarely left Solange's side. Another excellent student, Danielle seemed more friendly and open than Solange. She did not attract quite the same crowd of admirers, but she also wasn't as aloof. She looked at me from time to time at least, without wrinkling her nose. I'd have been glad to be friends with her. With her confident smile and short shiny brown hair, she struck me as even-keeled and lively.

From the start, I adored Sylvie. The other girls also admired her beauty. I wanted nothing more than to look like her, an absolute impossibility. Her round cheeks, blue eyes, and waist-length, rippling golden locks had nothing in common with my skinny face and short dark hair. Although she did not rank high in the class academically, she performed at an acceptable level and her warm smile and laughter drew many to her side. She did not speak to me, which would have been a social *faux pas*, but sometimes graced me with a smile. I never heard her mock me, as the others so often did, and I idolized her from afar.

Baggasin, meanwhile, stuck to me like a burr. As I became aware of the social hierarchy, her devotion made me uncomfortable. Where Solange floated above us all, Baggasin crawled in the muck. Backward and incapable, she never received even a *Bon Point*. *Incroyable!* She clearly came from a poor home, and her lack of cleanliness disgusted the other students. Although she was the only girl who'd ever made an effort to befriend me, I slowly came to the conclusion that spending time with Baggasin would only hinder my ability to make other friends.

The greatest trial of the day remained the long trek to the "other" school. The walk itself was not unpleasant, although as winter approached, we shivered when the wind bit at our bare legs. The agony lay in lining up in threes. I did my best to appear unconcerned, as though my position in the long line (always last) mattered not a bit to me. Solange always led, usually with Danielle at her side. I didn't care as much about my position in line as the nature of my companions. Occasionally, when it could be managed without being too obvious, I would slip into line next to two surprised girls just to avoid walking with Baggasin. I felt like a traitor, but somehow, I had to separate myself from her. Baggasin never rebuked me, just gazed at me with hurt eyes.

While I did not dare utter a word in my classmates' presence, I spoke French in my homework sessions with Marie-Laurence and Madame Wax. I could do no wrong in Madame Wax's eyes. I was always *adorable* and *mignonne*, which suited me fine. Marie-Laurence encouraged me and smiled her approval as I began to get my tongue around the strange French words.

Walking the eight blocks twice a day gave me a chance to overhear a lot of gossip: envy from the other girls about Solange's success or Sylvie's hair, concern about assignments, and, unfortunately, ridicule of me. Assuming I still couldn't understand a thing, they treated me like the village idiot, a source of ongoing mirth.

One afternoon, two girls flanked me and to my surprise took my arms and led me into the line for the walk back to our "home" school. I felt a brief flash of triumph. At last, someone other than Baggasin wanted to walk with me! Then I heard what they were saying.

"This will be a lark," said Sophie. The taller of the two, she still didn't come near my awkward stature.

"Yes, yes," said Pauline, tucking an auburn curl behind her ear, "let us see if she understands anything."

I smiled, a sour taste in my mouth.

"So Margarette," said Pauline sweetly, "Do you always splash ink all over yourself when you write? Is that the way they write in England?" They all thought that because I spoke English, I was from England. I had no way to correct them.

The girls in the row ahead turned to smirk at me. I stared ahead woodenly.

"But it looks so fashionable, so chic, the great splotches on her hands. Ooh la la." Sophie convulsed with laughter.

"They go so well with her fabulous *tablier*. I wonder, do you think she got it from her grandmother?"

The girls in the row behind us giggled too. Boiling inside, I continued to pretend I didn't understand a word.

"Where is your good friend Baggasin, Margarette? You are such a perfect pair. Maybe Baggasin can teach you to talk!" Pauline looked at me solemnly.

"I don't think anyone could teach her anything. She is, as Madame says, an idiot!"

I tried to close my ears, to sing a song in my head to distract myself. Since I sang poorly, this effort only demoralized me further. By the time we finally reached the old school and Madame bade us disperse home, hot tears burned the back of my eyes. Forgetting my posture of aloofness, I dashed out of the courtyard and ran all the way home.

My heart slowed as I turned the corner onto *rue Nicolet.* Here no one taunted me. In fact, I never saw my classmates outside of school. As far as I could tell, they never saw each other either. I'd never overheard them making plans or seen them leaving school together to walk home, the way I used to in Montreal West. A surprising number of parents, mostly mothers, waited for their daughters in the courtyard and accompanied them home. While this puzzled me, in the current situation it was a relief. Once free of school, I could breathe easily again and Josée and Patrick would soon be out to join me.

We got along famously on the street, but by some unspoken agreement, never acknowledged each other at school. I rarely saw Patrick, since the boys and girls were separated, but I did sometimes see Josée in the courtyard and in the line walking to and from the new school. She might smile shyly at me, but she never spoke. Nor did I, for some inner instinct told me that French girls who played on the street were not socially acceptable, and fond as I was of Josée, I was determined to scale the social ladder.

Fortunately, our in-school relationship did not affect our friendship on the street. We all behaved as though we had no idea that we attended the same school. Upon arrival at

6 rue Nicolet, I'd pop in and holler, "I'm home." My mother would encourage me to eat something; she still worried about my weight. I'd dutifully take a few bites of fruit or baguette, remove my *tablier,* and dash back outside. Josée and Patrick would be waiting for me, munching chunks of baguette sandwiching chocolate bars, true *pain au chocolate,* or perhaps it was the poor man's version of the Parisian pastry. The first time I saw them devouring their snacks, I stared. A chocolate sandwich? How very peculiar. But the longer I watched, the more appetizing it seemed. That night I begged my mother to let me have such a treat as my after-school snack. She shook her head with a *what in the world will they think of next* expression and told me it wasn't healthy. I pouted and wheedled, but on some matters my mother would not budge.

Pain au chocolate or not, sitting on the filthy curb with Josée and Patrick soothed my hurt spirits. By the time I had to go in for dinner, I felt revived and ready to attack my loathsome homework. I would learn French. I would memorize the inane passages. I would succeed. I fell asleep dreaming of the day I'd receive a *Grande Image* and my classmates would gather around murmuring *ooh la la.*

8

Désastre!

In early November, a nurse came to the school. We all lined up to receive something I took to be a vaccination. I clenched my teeth, fighting back my fear of needles, held out my arm and allowed the nurse to scrape the skin and apply a drop of liquid. Breathing again as I shuffled back to my seat, I felt a certain pride. Other girls sniffled and turned pale. Not me.

A week later, the nurse returned, and we jostled back into line so she could pull up our sleeves and examine the spot she'd scraped. Standing in my usual position towards the end of the line, my stomach knotted as I observed the girls ahead of me pulling up their sleeves to reveal smooth, unmarked skin. For the past week, I'd watched the scratch on my arm develop into an angry red swelling. My mother had said not to worry about it, she was sure it was a normal reaction. Now I could see she was terribly wrong and that, once again, I would stick out, the red welt on my arm a horrible contrast to their unblemished skin.

When my turn arrived, I pulled up the sleeve. The girls closest to me gasped. Their eyes widened and they muttered to each other. The nurse peered at my arm, then narrowed her eyes at me. *Madame la Maîtresse* gave me her *I knew you'd be trouble* look and shushed the girls. I tried to smile, as if to say, *no big deal, just a bit of swelling.*

Clearly, it was a big deal. *Madame la Maîtresse* told me to sit at a desk far from the lineup. The other girls huddled at some distance, watching me suspiciously. As soon as the nurse had viewed the final girl's arm, she hustled me away to an office. She held a muted conversation with *la principale de l'école*, who glowered at me as though I'd intentionally allowed my arm to swell up. The *principale* muttered something about *les Anglais* and marched from the room, leaving me with the chilly nurse. Half an hour later, my mother appeared, white-lipped.

"Come on, Meg." Her cheerfulness sounded forced. "I'm taking you home."

"Why?" Normally I'd be delighted by this turn of events, but this felt like a dismissal. Perhaps some rule forbade children with welts on their arms from attending school?

She didn't answer, just led me out of the office, through the courtyard, and out into the street.

"Mommy, what's going on? It's my vaccination, isn't it? None of the other girls had swelling. They seemed sort of scared when they saw my arm. What is it?"

I glanced up to see her eyes full of tears. She blinked them away and donned a wobbly smile. "Don't you worry, sweetie. I'll explain when we get home."

My heart pounded; I felt dizzy. Obviously, something was very wrong. The girls hadn't even laughed at me. They'd just watched with big eyes. I'd been so mortified to again find myself the centre of attention that I'd hardly noticed, but now snippets came back to me. They'd muttered things like *séjours loin*, stay away from her, and something to do with dying, *mourir*.

By the time we reached *rue Nicolet*, I'd begun to sniffle.

"Shh, shh," my mother murmured. "It'll be okay."

We climbed to the upper room. My father sat gazing out at the View.

"Hey, you're home earl—" He stopped short, taking in my mother's anxious face. "Margaret?"

"Sit down, honey." My mother guided me onto the couch.

"The school called," she said, her voice flat. "That vaccination—wasn't a vaccination. It was a TB test. Meg tested positive."

"Positive?" My dad's face went white.

"What's a TB test?" I asked.

"A test for tuberculosis," my mother whispered. "It's a … an illness."

"Like tonsillitis?"

She nodded. "Yes, sort of like that. That may be why you've been so tired, the fevers, the lack of appetite …" She glanced at my father.

He nodded.

"So? What is it? What—?" I glanced from one to the other, not liking anything about this. They looked so frightened.

"It's … pretty rare these days," said my mother. "I don't know. We have to take you to a doctor and find out what it means."

"The American hospital," said my father. "We'll go there."

My mother nodded. "Yes." She sounded relieved. I could understand. At least they'd be able to talk to the doctors there in English. "I'll set that up right away. You won't be able to go to school until the doctor says it's okay."

This sounded just fine to me, but ... "Why? Is this TB catching?"

They looked at each other again.

"We don't know," said my mother, "but maybe."

"Can I go out and play with Patrick and Josée?"

"They're still in school, honey," said my mother. "Besides, you don't want them to get sick, do you?"

"I'm not sick!" I wailed.

My father gestured for me to come sit in his lap. I scurried over. He held me close. "It'll be okay, Meggie."

That afternoon, he took me for a walk and bought me a strawberry tart, which cheered me only a little.

When we got home, my mother's eyes looked red, but she seemed calm. "We've got an appointment on Thursday."

"Good, good," my father declared brightly.

They poured drinks, despite the early hour. As they drank in uncomfortable silence, my thoughts whirled back to the days in Montreal West when I'd been forced to stay in bed all weekend. I recalled the endless visits to antiseptic doctors' offices where I had to take off my clothes and sit shivering on cots covered in paper, the parade of doctors who prodded me and made me stick out my tongue and gag. I'd never been to a hospital, but I figured it must just be a whole bunch of doctors' offices and rooms full of people dying.

We had a quiet evening. My parents told Frances and Neil about the positive TB test. Frances disappeared down to our bedroom. Neil tried to make jokes. Nobody laughed. I went to bed feeling chilly inside. Frances, usually so distant in that three-quarter bed, hugged me for a long time. It didn't lift my spirits.

In the morning, I felt fine. I slipped out into rainy darkness and honking cars. People crowding the *boulangerie* smiled at me and the lady behind the counter patted me on the head as she handed over the baguettes. Cradling the warm bread as I walked home, I chuckled to myself. Surely everyone had over-reacted. I felt fine. Parents. They worried too much. I would not let it get to me.

On Thursday, the long car ride to the hospital bored me stiff, as did the waiting inside the big shiny building. It was *jeudi* after all. We should have been having fun, doing something. I tried to ignore the little knot in my tummy.

The young doctor spoke English, drawling his words in a way that reminded me of my grandmother. Clearly American. I couldn't follow much of what he said but he got my full attention when he said "Now, Meg, we have to take some blood."

"What do you mean?" I cried, imagining a quick knife slash to my arm and blood pouring out.

"Shh, it's okay," murmured my mother.

No, it's not, I thought, and over the next several months I became increasingly suspicious of such assurances, as they invariably preceded my worst fear: needles.

We walked down a brightly lit hall to another steely clean office where a nurse awaited us. I found it hard to breathe.

"Hi Meg," she said.

"Hi," I muttered, gazing desperately at my mother.

"Why don't you just sit down and relax?" She indicated a large chair with wide leather arms.

My mother shepherded me into the chair. I dug my fingers into her arm as she attempted to withdraw.

"It'll be all right. Over in a flash," she lied, prying my fingers away.

I felt dizzy.

"Now we're going to extract the blood from your arm," said the nurse.

"No!" I howled.

My mother's face had this way of tightening into something like a grimace when she was trying to be firm or brave and wasn't really feeling that way. I recognized the expression; my panic increased.

The nurse smiled and patted my arm, almost distracting me with her bright blonde curls. People with needles shouldn't be allowed to be pretty. "It won't take long and it doesn't really hurt."

Having given up on my mother, I cast a piteous glance at my father. His face didn't look any better, all scrunched and furrowed, but he attempted a grin.

"Daddy, I don't WANT this. I'm scared!"

He nodded appreciatively. Big help.

"Meg, no one likes needles," said the nurse, who didn't seem so pretty anymore. "But it's the only way we can find out how sick you are."

"I'm not sick!" I protested.

She took a needle from the table—a needle with a huge glass bottle attached to it—and moved towards me. My mother held my hand, making soothing noises, and told me to close my eyes. I decided this was the smartest suggestion she'd made all day and did so.

A ferocious pain jabbed my arm, right in the tender crook. I shrieked. My mother clutched my hand. The pain continued. My head swam.

"There. All done," said the nurse.

I opened my eyes. Black spots ballooned on the walls. The floor buckled.

"Breathe deeply." The nurse sounded anxious. "Here, lean forward. Put your head between your knees." She applied pressure to the back of my head, and I bent over.

Slowly the floor stopped moving. Breathless and clammy, I muttered, "I think I'm going to be sick," but as I sat in that awkward position, the feeling faded.

"Next time, we'll make sure she's lying down," the nurse murmured.

Next time? I closed my eyes again.

"How're you doing, honey?" my mother asked softly.

"Okay, I guess. Can we go home now?"

No response. I raised my head.

"Not quite yet." The nurse smiled brightly. "We have to take some x-rays."

I breathed again. I'd had x-rays in Montreal, when they were trying to figure out why I kept running a fever. X-rays didn't hurt.

I wobbled to my feet. My mother put her arm around me and my father patted my shoulder. The three of us followed the nurse back down the hall into an elevator, along more halls, into a room where they turned the lights off and told me not to breathe. Then *click,* it was over.

"You can go home now," said yet another nurse.

I heaved a sigh of relief as the doors of the hospital swung closed behind us. In the car I asked, "So? Is everything okay?"

"Well, yes. I mean it's better than we thought." My mother said.

"The hospital will call when they get the results, but you're going to be okay." My dad grinned at me in the rearview mirror.

I relaxed and fell asleep.

That evening, my parents explained that the doctor needed to confirm I actually had TB. My heart lifted.

"So maybe I don't have it after all? It was just a mistake?"

"Maybe." My mother sounded dubious. "But even if you have TB, they can treat it. You won't have to go to a hospital."

"Or a sanatorium," my sister piped up.

My mother frowned at her in a *keep quiet* way.

"A what?" I asked. The word had an ominous ring.

"A sanatorium. It's a hospital especially for people with TB." My father sipped his drink.

"In the mountains usually," Frances added. "Aunt Joan spent time in one, didn't she, Dad?"

My mother's frown deepened.

My father gave a quick nod and looked away. I vaguely remembered talk of my wee Aunt Joan being ill as a child and having to go away for a long time to recover. Given that there were no mountains in Paris, apart from the small one on which our house perched, I didn't like the sound of this at all.

"Anyway, they now have drugs you can take," said my mother firmly. "if you need them." Then she changed the subject.

In the end, we had to go back to the hospital for more tests. I protested to no avail. The blood test, which they assured me would not be repeated, showed I definitely had tuberculosis, but the x-ray did not show any sign of it in my chest.

"Maybe that's why they couldn't figure it out in Montreal," my mother said.

The doctors poked me and sent me to more rooms with big machines. I lay on my back while the machines clicked. I began to think longingly of school. At least it would be a reprieve from sitting around waiting to hear from doctors who might want more of my blood.

My mother laughed when I asked her about it. "You want to go back?"

"No, not really. I just wondered." It would hardly do to backtrack on my stance.

On our next trip to the hospital, the doctor looked pleased. "It's in her stomach glands," he announced.

"TB? In her stomach glands?" My mother looked indignant.

"Yes! It's peculiar, unusual. But it's not contagious." He smiled.

"And the treatment? Will she ... will she need to ... stay here?"

"No, no!" The doctor wrote on a little pad. "She just has to take medication. Two pills a day." He tore off the sheet with a flourish and handed it to my mother. "You can get it filled at the dispensary downstairs."

"Good! Thank you!" My father rose.

"Wait a minute, Bill," said my mother.

He sank down again.

"For how long?" she asked the doctor.

"What?"

"How long does she have to take the medication for?"

"Oh." The doctor nodded as though she were a particularly bright student. "Yes. Good point. It's not an easy disease to treat, as you know. It's critical that she complete the entire course. We'll need to see her every month to monitor her progress, but generally speaking patients stay on the medication for two years."

My mother's eyebrows shot up. "Two years!"

The doctor nodded gravely then brightened. "But you're going to be just fine, Meg. Not to worry."

A doomed piece of advice. The thought of taking pills every day for two years, not to mention returning to the hospital every month, had me very worried.

"So, she can go back to school?" my mother continued.

"Absolutely! What do you think of that, Meg?"

I stared at the floor, suddenly uncertain. I didn't want to be sick or have to stay at the hospital a moment longer than necessary, but now that I obviously would be returning to school, my former anxieties rose. Being branded an imbecile and a foreigner—indeed an enemy, as France and England had always been at war (and in our history book, the English were clearly the bad guys)—had been bad enough. Now I was a diseased foreign imbecile. I could just imagine how my classmates would welcome me back. It could only be a *désastre*!

9

Americans in Paris

Absorbed in my own small world, I paid little attention to my siblings' affairs. Neil and I had never been close, largely because of our age difference. Eight years seemed an immense gap and we had little in common. It didn't help that in Montreal West he had tended to act as my tormentor. A born prankster, he'd often cast me as his unwitting dupe. One April Fools' Day, he'd woven an elaborate conspiracy in which the two of us would make fun of my sister's suspicious nature. He'd offer her a glass of ginger ale, she'd refuse it, suspecting foul play, and I would make a fool of her by drinking it down. I complied only to find myself drinking a glass full of dishwashing liquid. My parents were not at all amused when they had to rush me to the hospital. Nor was I.

Contrariwise, I'd always been close to Frances. I thought her the most brilliant beautiful girl in the world. She'd coddled me as a child and bought me the only chocolate Easter bunny I'd ever had. (My parents thought coloured hard-boiled eggs sufficient for Easter hunts. When I found the chocolate bunny from Frances, it was like finding a pot of gold at the end of a rainbow.) Once she entered her teenage years, she tried to distance herself from her little sister, but I still idolized her.

In Paris, we lived in different worlds. My siblings left earlier in the morning than I did and returned close to dinnertime; their metro ride took over an hour each way. Their teachers spoke French and their homework seemed to be every bit as challenging as mine, but they had English-speaking classmates. I could tell from the amount of time Frances spent curling her hair and fussing about her clothes that she wanted to impress the boys. I couldn't imagine why; boys struck me as noisy, dirty, and obnoxious, and I felt relieved that my class was all girls. When I asked Frances about it, she rolled her eyes and said, "You wouldn't understand."

When she first mentioned a boy named Berry, I assumed she'd fallen in love and began plotting ways to tease her. But she didn't seem smitten, just enthusiastic, and the fact that she talked to my parents about him forced me to revise my opinion. When Frances experienced romantic feelings for boys, she didn't tell my parents. She wrote about it in her diary. Or at least I assumed that's what she was doing as she scrawled secretively in that peculiar little book, sighing and gazing into space. Once I started to open it just to have a look, but she snatched it from me and shouted, "That's private."

Nonetheless, she couldn't stop talking about this Berry and his family.

"They're so unusual, Mom," Frances enthused. "Berry plays recorder and his brother plays the flute and they're studying with really top people, and he has a little sister, must be about Meg's age, who paints really well."

"What's her name?" I interrupted.

Frances stared at me blankly, as though she'd forgotten my presence. "Oh...uh... Becky, I think." She turned back to my parents. "Anyway, they lived in Puerto Rico before they moved to Paris, and they live in Montmartre too! They've been here a couple of years and they know lots of other Americans. Berry and I think you should meet."

"They sound interesting, honey," said my mother.

"Yes. Wouldn't it be fun to have some American friends?"

"Hmmm. Yes. That would be nice." My mother didn't sound convinced.

I thought it funny that my sister would attempt to make friends for my parents. Didn't she know it worked the other way around? No wonder my parents were uncomfortable with the idea.

Not long after, my sister succeeded in her matchmaking. This didn't surprise me; Frances could talk anyone into anything. Given that the Haywards invited us to their house, I suspected Berry was a co-conspirator.

We walked to their place early one evening. Glittering raindrops dotted the steamy windows of shops and cafés. Delicious aromas from restaurants floated on the air. We wandered the narrow cobblestoned streets, Frances and Neil leading, then my parents, with me trailing just behind them. My mother seemed nervous.

"It could be a little awkward, don't you think?" she murmured to my dad. "We really know nothing about these people."

"It's an evening out, with Americans!" My father tucked her hand under his arm and patted it. "If we don't get along, we don't have to see them again. It'll be fine, Margaret."

"I suppose you're right." Her face relaxed and she smiled, her eyes twinkling. She wore lipstick and a soft red dress under her trim raincoat. We arrived at a modern-looking apartment building, an anomaly in Paris. Frances led us into a tiny elevator; we crammed in and I held my breath as it jerked and rattled its way up two floors. We knocked at a door and it burst open to reveal a most unusual family, all diminutive, wide-eyed, and grinning. The father, confusingly also named Berry, stood only an inch or two taller than my small mother. His wife Ruth was bone-thin and quite a bit shorter; I'd never seen such a small adult. She had long straight black hair tied in a ponytail and huge dark eyes lined in black. Big Berry, as they called him despite his stature, had a mass of curly dark hair, impish eyes and skin the colour of Josée and Patrick's. The three children had inherited their parents' size and enthusiasm.

They greeted us as though we were long lost cousins, hugging and kissing us and talking in loud voices. Then they led us into the large apartment. Thick Persian rugs covered not just the floor, but the couches. Colourful paintings adorned the walls and billowing paisley material draped the windows. All the furniture sat close to the floor: carved stools, low-slung chairs with thick cushions. A mass of candles flickered on the large coffee table and the air smelled spicy. Later my mother would describe it as *bohemian*.

Until meeting the Haywards, I'd always thought, and had indeed been told by friends, that my family was loud. In contrast to this boisterous group, we seemed restrained. They burbled with excitement, about how wonderful it was to meet us, how charming we were, how interesting.

The adults settled on the low furniture with glasses of wine. Becky dragged me off to her room and proceeded to show me her paintings and drawings. I felt awed. Her pictures looked like real art, with fantastic images in vivid colours. She told me all about her family. Her mother was a psycho-analyst who used to dance at night clubs in New York until Berry rescued her. With Ruth being Jewish and Berry part black, they'd suffered a lot of discrimination, so they'd left the States to live in Puerto Rico, which had been fabulous. Paris, Becky assured me breathlessly, was even better. The artistic community was vibrant, and Ruth and Berry had really found their niche and they supported their children's artistic endeavours and loved the intellectual ambiance of Parisian life.

I blinked at this round-faced, beaming girl, dressed in a leotard and long skirt. She talked like a grown-up. But she was exactly my age and she spoke English! She chattered on, seeming delighted with my company despite my near silence. She loved Paris, spoke perfect French, and went to an American *école* right next to the *lycée* that our older siblings attended. I sighed. She was so lucky.

We gathered around the coffee table to eat. I thought it great fun to have a vast coffee table set like a real table, with all of us sitting on cushions on the floor. The conversations continued at a fever pitch. My father and Big Berry discussed education and sociology-like things. Frances and Little Berry talked about school. Neil chatted with the middle child, Chris, about music. Becky and I got quite chummy, but most of the time everyone engaged in the same conversation, talking over each other and laughing a lot. When we finally stumbled out, they made us promise to get together again soon.

"They're so lively!" said my mother, as we walked home. My father, rosy from wine, chortled. "It's amazing. Berry's working for the OECD, you know. He's got some fascinating ideas."

Despite her reservations, my mother had clearly enjoyed the contact with people from home.

"But they came from Puerto Rico, not Canada," I said.

"Yes, but they are American," said my mother.

Although I'd lived my whole life in Canada, both my siblings had been born in Chicago and my parents had retained not just their American citizenship, but their loyalty to all things American. This became especially clear a few days later.

We'd just finished dinner. Or rather everyone else had. My mother, determined to master French cuisine in the course of our stay, had produced a meat dish with a rich sauce that raised my suspicions.

"Is it horse meat?" I knew the French ate horse meat, a truly horrific habit, and would not put it past my adventurous mother to disguise it with a sauce.

"No, of course not," she sniffed. "It's *Boeuf Bourguignon*. But really, we must get over our disapproval of horse meat. What's the real difference between horse meat and beef?"

"I'm not hungry." I scowled.

No doubt one of our interminable arguments would have broken out if the phone hadn't rung.

My father answered it. "Oh hi, Berry, how are—What?" He sat down abruptly. "Oh no, no. When …?"

My mother rose to hover at his shoulder.

"Yes. Okay. Thank you." He returned the receiver to its cradle and rose. "The president has been shot," he said. He stumbled across the living room to the radio.

My mother teetered and sat down. "What do you mean? Shot? By who? That can't be right. Why would anyone shoot him? Was that Berry?"

"Yes, Berry. They just heard." He fiddled with the dials on the radio, "Damn this thing!"

My mother didn't upbraid him for swearing. She hurried to the radio too. The big brown box squeaked and squawked.

"Go more slowly," my mother murmured.

My father glared.

I felt frightened. I knew nothing about politics except that John F. Kennedy was president. His election had been a cause for celebration, because he was a Democrat, like my parents. I also got the impression they liked the fact that he was young, although he didn't look all that young to me. He reminded me of my father. And he had a glamorous wife named Jackie, who wore short dresses and little hats. He was very important, the President after all.

My parents muttered as they tried to find news on the radio. Finally, an American voice came through. We sat in silence, craning to hear the announcer amidst the crackling of the radio. The light faded in the room.

"Three shots fired at the president's motorcade ... Dallas ... attempted assassination ... Mrs. Kennedy shouted 'No'... motorcade kept moving ... Hospital ... top surgeons summoned ... Roman Catholic priests ... still alive ... in critical condition."

My sister sniffled on the couch. Neil paced. My mother shook her head. "It can't be." My father looked grim. I'd never seen my family so quiet.

The radio announcers seemed to be arguing, uncertain about whether the president had died or not. They talked about bulletins and CBS and Columbia and trouble getting through, circuits being busy.

We continued to sit there, waiting. I wanted to cry myself, even though I didn't know the president. I felt so sad for my parents. They didn't know him either, but he meant so much to them.

"I wish we were at home," said my mother. "It feels so far away."

My father nodded, his head close to the radio.

I wondered why it would be better to be closer. I guess they'd have been able to hear better or watch on TV.

Then, briefly, the announcer's voice came through with perfect clarity. "It's confirmed. The president is dead, of a gunshot wound to the head. Mrs. Kennedy was not injured. Police have arrested a young man. Vice President Lyndon Johnson will be sworn in …"

My father leaned back. No one spoke.

10

Asinine Play

I returned to school, grim and determined, once I'd started the TB medication. As expected, the girls gave me a wide berth in the courtyard. As we lined up, no one wanted to walk with me. Old faithful Baggasin, perhaps unaware of my pariah status, grinned and joined me, but no third girl had any intention of coming near. *Madame la Maîtresse* seized an unfortunate by the collar of her *tablier* and shoved her next to me in the line. Then she called the class to attention.

"Margarette is not dangerous," she pronounced. Her steely glance in my direction nonetheless suggested I'd committed an unpardonable crime by becoming ill. "She is not infectious. You cannot get sick from her. Now, let us go. I expect no more nonsense from any of you." Again, she held my gaze, as though the remark were intended for me alone.

Everyone stared at me and the girls whispered among themselves all the way to the other school, but soon I faded from their consciousness again. I crowed to myself. *Such cowards, afraid of a silly little illness.* (Not that it seemed so silly when, each morning, I had to force down two gigantic pills. After a number of hysterical scenes, in which I gagged and threw up, my mother resorted to grinding them up and mixing them with chocolate milk. Needless to say, this did not improve the flavour of that already vile drink.)

Although I still spoke not a word at school, I chattered away to Josée and Patrick when we met on the street in the late afternoon. As winter approached, darkness fell early and we played among the growing shadows and the thin light of streetlamps. Even with the chill, I loved this playtime. The tall bare-branched trees and scuttling clouds gave an air of mystery to our games. I imagined us as spies and thieves, something out of *The Highwayman* perhaps. Early in our relationship, despite my poor French, I'd established myself as the ringleader, a role I always tended to take. In Montreal West, I'd directed the games of Pretend, playing the leader (mother, doctor, circus master), digging into my mother's bin of old clothes for costumes and assigning roles and props to my younger friends.

Initially, Josée and Patrick were a little puzzled when I tried to engage them in such games. Our communication took the form of charades, with me miming and them trying to figure out my meaning. We began, naturally, playing School. I pointed at myself and declared, "*Madame la Maîtresse.*"

They giggled and looked blank.

"*Étudiants!*" I announced, pointing at them.

It took a little while, but they caught on. We drew desks and blackboards in the air and took our appointed positions. I ordered them to recite their *resumés*. Josée shyly gabbled something I assumed she'd learned for class and I variously shouted "*Imbecile!*" or patted her head and handed her an invisible *Bon Point*. I made them march around the block holding hands. Patrick objected because girls and boys wouldn't walk together. When I suggested he could pretend to be a girl, he crossed his arms over his small chest indignantly. Josée, however, didn't mind the idea of playing a boy and strutted about quite convincingly. When Patrick asked if he could be *Le Maître*, I lost interest and changed the game, now taking the part of Zorro and flicking an invisible sword in a "z" motion. They stared at me, bewildered. It seemed Zorro was not well known in Paris.

As my French improved, I coaxed them to play more complex scenarios. A favourite was for Patrick and me to play pirates, out to kidnap Josée. We'd skulk about in doorways, waiting and saying "Arrrr" a lot. Josée would trip down the street like Little Red Riding Hood, all innocent and carefree, and we'd leap out and chase her up our street and down another. Once we caught her, no difficult feat given that she was so small, we'd "tie" her up and mutter dreadful threats related to walking the plank. (I loved the Peter Pan story.) She'd pretend fear but ultimately spoil the entire game by laughing.

I loved these imaginary pursuits, even if my playmates didn't take them as seriously as I did. When it started to get dark very early, my mother wanted me to come inside after barely half an hour of play.

"But Mom," I moaned, "there's nothing to do inside! I want to play with my friends!"

"Well, if they'd just come into the house, you could," she sniffed.

But I knew Josée and Patrick would not come in. I wondered why. Perhaps they had a cruel stepmother who hoped they would starve to death out on the street and didn't want them entering a nice warm home where they might get a treat.

"Mom, can I just go out and ask Josée one question?"

"No," my mother sighed. "You can ask her tomorrow."

The next day, Madame announced that our class would be preparing a *pièce pour Noël*. I didn't get it. A piece for Christmas? A piece of what? Pie? Cake? Then, as she rattled on about the birth of Jesus and *le spectacle* and Marie and Joseph and *les rois*, I understood. We'd be doing a play, a Christmas play!

In Montreal West, at the church where my mother insisted we attend Sunday School (while my father rolled his eyes and sank behind his book), we had done a Christmas pageant. I'd been an angel, one of the very little ones. My mother had sewn me a pair of beautiful gauzy wings. It had been exciting, performing at night in the old church with lit candles and the faint scent of pine in the air. I didn't have to say anything, I'd been too little then, but now...

Madame began to cast my classmates in their roles. Of course, Solange was Mary; she had a lovely clear voice and great poise. Sylvie of the golden locks would be the main angel. Perfect casting, I could not deny. When Madame announced that Danielle would play Joseph, she wrinkled her nose and complained that she wouldn't get to wear a pretty gown. *But at least she had a speaking role.* A speaking role. My shoulders slumped. I couldn't have a speaking role, because as far as anyone knew, I couldn't speak.

For a moment I considered breaking my vow of silence, just so I could be in the play. If they could see me act, I thought, their attitude towards me would change. I gave my head a shake, barely hearing the names of those who would be wise men and shepherds. I couldn't start speaking now. I'd look desperate and besides I would *not* open my mouth until I was word perfect.

By now almost everyone had a part and Madame explained that the rest of us would be *les animaux*. Animals! I felt a grim frown settle on my face and tried to smooth it away. No point in letting my irritation show. But really. Animals!

She began with the sheep. That wouldn't be too bad, to frolic about as a pretty little lamb. I tried to imagine a lamb's costume: curly white wool would be quite attractive. But no, the smallest of the remaining (and obviously inferior) girls got the parts of the cute little lambs. The camel would be played by Nicole and Sophie. I sniggered silently. Who'd want to be a great galumphing camel with a hump? Then I looked around. All the girls who'd been assigned their roles had lined up at the front of the room. Only Baggasin and I remained seated. Ominous.

Madame smiled at us. At least I think she smiled; it looked more like a thin grimace. Then she announced, with too much relish, I thought, that Baggasin and I would be *l'âne*. It took me a minute or two to figure out what the word meant. The girls giggled, watching me with nasty little faces, waiting to see me burst into tears. Baggasin grinned, showing dirty teeth, and mimed donkey ears, no doubt in an attempt to help me understand. The giggles became full-fledged guffaws.

I was to be half of a donkey. *Incroyable*. How much worse could life get? I tried to laugh it off, which probably made me look lunatic. I didn't care. All my joy at the thought of being in a play dissolved.

Next the girls discussed their costumes. Madame informed us that we would have to supply our own costumes. I could just imagine my mother's reaction. Although she loved to cook, she was not very domestic. Apart from the angel wings, which she'd created from a pattern, the only time she'd ever made a costume for me was when I'd marched in a Santa Claus parade as a candy cane. Marched might be overstating the matter. Stuck inside a cardboard tube with red and white stripes, I'd barely been able to move. At one point I toppled over and had to be lifted back onto my feet. No one even recognized me as a candy cane. Now I dreaded what my mother might do to make me look like half a donkey.

"That's great," she said. "You don't have to learn any lines."

My brother chimed in. "Except hee-haw. How would you say that in French? Haw-hee?" He doubled up laughing. Cretin.

"It is NOT great. It's ridiculous. What can I possibly wear?" I glared at Neil.

"Oh, that shouldn't be a problem." My mother put on her thinking look. "An old blanket would work, cover up the fact that there are two of you. Are you the front or the back?"

This critical question had not been decided, but I suddenly realized that if I were the back, no one would know it was me. "The back!" I declared, knowing Baggasin would agree to whatever I wanted.

"So you'll be the ass of the ass!" Neil roared with laughter.

"Neil!" My mom sounded a lot sterner than she looked. Was she laughing too?

I clumped down to my room and tried to imagine I was an all-powerful magician turning my brother into a toad.

Rehearsals began. Needless to say, the donkey did not have a lot to do. Solange, as Mary, thought it would be cute to ride on our backs. Fortunately, Madame regarded this as "*trop compliqué.*"

Initially, Baggasin resisted the notion, communicated by me in a dazzling mime, of taking on the front end of the donkey; she was by nature more follower than leader. However, when I insisted, her eyes grew large and she nodded, apparently thrilled that she'd be able to show her face. That decided, we spent rehearsals either shuffling along beside Solange and Danielle or sitting on the sidelines.

I watched the *pièce* develop with disgust. The girls spoke their lines the same way they recited *resumés*, intoning without expression, with the exception of Solange and Danielle. I had to admit they put some spirit into their roles. Madame hardly qualified as a *directeur de théâtre*. I found her *mise en scène* uninspired. The girls shuffled on and off, frequently bumping into each other and giggling.

As we neared our performance, a mishmash of costumes appeared. Each sheep looked different, some wrapped in shawls or blankets, others in moth-eaten fur coats. Solange wore a lovely blue velvet dress, Danielle a man's white shirt, much too large for her, and a blanket as a cape. The entire affair stuck me as ludicrous and incompetent, without any of the magic of Christmas or the theatre.

My family, Madame Wax and Marie-Laurence insisted on attending the performance. I begged them to stay at home.

"But Meg," said my mother, "we want to support you."

I frowned. "It will be embarrassing."

"It's just a play," she said soothingly, "and we want to see it."

83

The performance took place not by candlelight on a snowy evening, but at the school on a grey afternoon. I felt every inch an ass under the hot, itchy brown blanket. Baggasin looked like an idiot with droopy ears made from crumpled brown paper. She seemed incapable of paying attention. I had to poke her in the bum, which gave me some satisfaction, to prod her into action for each of our three cues. On the third, she let out a shriek and jerked forward, pulling the blanket with her. I found myself exposed, my face red and sweaty, before an audience rocking with laughter. Even my mother smiled. I scrambled back under the blanket, cursing Madame and *Noël* and bloody Baggasin in a furious whisper.

The next time I acted, I vowed, I would play nothing less than a queen.

11

Noël

I could hardly wait for *les vacances de Noël,* when I'd have two full weeks off school!

My parents had planned the year to include trips to different parts of Europe. Whatever their shortcomings, French schools provided generous holidays. In late October we'd traveled to Holland for a week. The incessant rain dampened our spirits, but the canals in Amsterdam and the wooden clogs delighted me. I spent hours imagining myself as the boy with his finger in the dyke or the little match girl, pining piteously in a ragged dress. We visited a gallery with paintings by the mad artist Vincent van Gogh, who cut off his own ear; his swirling pictures and tragic life captured my imagination. My parents bought me a small doll dressed in traditional Dutch costume, the start of a collection, they promised. I'd never been a huge fan of dolls, but I loved the costume: the wide white-winged cap, the apron and coloured skirt, the clogs.

For Christmas, we planned to head south, to Spain. It didn't seem right to me that we would be in a warm, possibly even hot, country for the holiday. It never snowed in Paris and my Tennessee-born mother fancied a warm Christmas rather than a grey one. I longed for snow and all the trimmings of a traditional Christmas. To appease me (and probably everyone else) my father bought a miniature tree, not even a proper pine tree, but something similar. We decorated it with small twinkle lights and a few delicate French ornaments, satin-covered balls with tassels. At home my mother always made gingerbread men that we decorated with coloured icing and sprinkles and hung on our tree. When I asked about whether we'd have them here, my mother frowned.

"I don't know that we can. No one seems to bake at home here. They just buy things at the *pâtisserie*."

"But we HAVE to have gingerbread boys," I wailed. It wouldn't be Christmas without them.

My mother pursed her lips. "I'll see," she said.

I hounded her about them and finally, at quite ridiculous expense, she found most of the ingredients, except for cookie cutters.

"We should have brought them." I stamped my foot.

"Well, we didn't," she snapped back.

My mother hand-carved the gingerbread boys, who all looked a bit wobbly, like something van Gogh might have created. As we had no food colouring for the icing, they also lacked the bright colours of the gingerbread boys we'd decorated in Montreal West. "They'll have to do," my mother sighed.

We held a festive dinner a week before Christmas, just before we left. As our tiny oven couldn't hold a turkey, my mother had the *boucher* cook it for us. She substituted squash for sweet potatoes; I liked neither so refused that dish. Overall it was a lovely little supper and we sang some carols and exchanged very modest presents. The Haywards roared into our small house and even Madame Wax and Marie-Laurence dropped in for a few minutes, perching uncomfortably on the antique furniture. After our semi-American feast, we prepared for our trip.

On a chilly dark morning, the five of us squeezed into the little Volkswagen. I sat in the middle of the back seat, cramped between Neil and Frances. We drove south, forever it seemed, through cold damp weather.

"It'll be warm when we reach the Riviera," my mother promised. She talked longingly about the Mediterranean and Marseille and Nice, where rich people vacationed, lounging on white sand beaches in expensive bathing suits.

At last we reached the Mediterranean and for one night booked into a modest hotel overlooking the sea. When we awoke in the morning, we stared out the window, disoriented. A thin blanket of snow covered the beaches. At breakfast we learned it was the coldest winter they'd experienced on the Riviera in forty years.

"Just our luck," grumbled my father.

We pushed on, driving west and then south into the snow-capped Pyrenees Mountains on the border of France and Spain. The twisting roads had my mother gasping and clutching the door handle, as though that would save her if we tumbled down a steep incline.

"The Pyrenees!" I shouted in glee. Then I proceeded to recite, on a rising note to its triumphant conclusion, one of the *resumés* I'd learned for school.

"*Dans une guerre contre les Saracens / Roland, neveu de Charlemagne / Est mort en Col de Roncevaux/ Dans les Pyrénées!*" (In a war against the Saracens, Roland, nephew of Charlemagne, died in the Pass of Roncesvalles, in the Pyrenees.)

Initially my mother applauded. The whole family had heard me practising this engaging ditty for some days prior to delivering it in class. They made appreciative noises: my history lesson had come in handy. By the time I'd chanted it twenty times, my siblings were shouting "Shut up!" I continued to mutter it under my breath. They cast baleful glances at me as the weary hours of white-knuckle driving wore on.

We arrived in Barcelona late in the day. No snow covered the beaches or boardwalk, but the air remained cool. We checked into a hotel, where I had to share a room with both my siblings. (Frances objected loudly to this cramped state of affairs.) Then we set off to find some dinner. None of us spoke Spanish. My parents had a phrase book and attempted, with considerable effort, to explain our mission to the *señor* at the hotel desk. Spaniards apparently spoke no more English than Parisians, so they resorted to mime. My father pointed at his mouth, my mother made fork and knife gestures, pretending to sit at an invisible table. They repeated "*res-toe-**ron**-tay*" in louder and louder voices. The Spanish gentlemen looked a bit irritated, but led us to the door and gestured, seeming to suggest there might be a restaurant up the street. Perhaps around the corner?

We smiled and nodded and started out the door.

"No," he said, shaking his head and pointing at his watch.
"What do you think he means?" asked my mother.
"Maybe he wants the time," murmured my dad. He yelled, "It's just after 6 o'clock."
The desk man frowned.
"He must know what time it is," said my mother. "He has a watch."
My brother and sister giggled.
"Well, let's just go. I'm starving," said my father.
Nodding and smiling, we stepped out of the hotel into the dark city. We made our way up the cobblestone street into a square full of lit trees. Not fir trees, just ordinary trees, barren of leaves, with strings of white fairy lights wound around their spreading branches.
We stopped and stared.
"How beautiful," said my mother.
The lights, the gentle air and the silence struck me as positively magical. Tinkerbell or Rumplestiltskin might pop out from a dark alley near the square at any moment.
"Look," said Neil, who was always starving. "Isn't that a restaurant?"
It looked like one, with a big window, awning, and menu. But no welcoming light shone from inside the small building. We peered in at shadowy tables, but saw no food, no waiters.
"It's not open." My father voiced the obvious.
"Maybe some of the restaurants close over Christmas," said my mom.
We trudged on, puzzled. Light spilled from shops. People, dark-haired and loud-voiced, entered to the sounds of little bells and emerged carrying parcels, but the promising signs with the word *Restaurante* only adorned darkened buildings.

We tried stopping people to ask, saying "*Restaurante*" in increasingly desperate tones. No one spoke English. They waved towards the dark buildings and scurried away. Finally, my mother spied a little sign on a door, which read "21.00", 9 o'clock.

"Maybe they don't open until later," said my mother.

"9 o'clock? That's ridiculous," grumbled my dad. "Meg should be in bed by nine!"

Eventually we found a *taberna*, a bar full of smoke and noisy men, where we huddled at a table and managed to order dry, heavy bread and a plate of greasy salami and olives. My parents drank wine. We children got Fanta, a very fizzy version of Orange Crush. We all munched the tasteless bread. The black olives proved very disappointing, strong and salty, not at all like the fleshy ones we got in cans at home.

Apparently even nine o'clock was regarded as early to dine in Spain. This threw my parents into quite a state. The sickly girl had to get to bed by a decent time, but she also had to eat! Much to my irritation, more often than not they rustled up some not-particularly-appealing evening meal (sandwich-like) that I ate in the room, prior to going to bed. Then the rest of the family went out to eat around 10:00 PM, leaving a grumpy Neil or Frances to babysit me. While I resented being forced to eat in my room like a baby, I didn't mind missing dinners in restaurants. I found Spanish food unappealing: saltless bread and tons of fish and seafood. My parents raved about the paella. It just tasted fishy to me.

I liked Barcelona because the entire city seemed to be on holiday at Christmastime. Through the shuttered hotel window, I heard people carousing outside until almost dawn.

In the morning, the streets were deserted. People would emerge for a little while around noon before withdrawing for their siestas. As one who'd been forced to nap for too many years, I rather liked being in a country where everyone rested after lunch! After dark, the city sprang to life. People strolled through the plazas under the gorgeous light-strung trees. Warm breezes picked up the scents of exotic flowers, gentle waves lapped at the beaches. We wandered along the boardwalk; I watched the harbour in case an exotic traveller like Gulliver or Aladdin should sail in.

The highlight of our Barcelona stay was New Year's Eve. My parents arranged for us all—even me—to attend a special banquet in a castle, with a performance by flamenco dancers. The beautiful women swishing their skirts and clicking their castanets enthralled me. I felt almost like a queen, sitting in a richly decorated hall, with gold goblets and plates, in a castle overlooking the city. I suspect everyone else had a little to drink that night. My sixteen-year-old brother liked the flamenco dancers every bit as much as I did and kept shouting "*Olé*" and trying to get up on the stage with them. My mother "now Neil"ed him back into his seat. The music, flashing smiles, and clacking heels got me so excited that I actually stayed awake until midnight.

Before we left Spain, my parents bought me a costume doll of a flamenco dancer. She became the star of my eventually sizable collection. I can still see her long curly dark hair and flounced yellow dress, cut high at the front to show off her perfect legs and low at the bust. In the quiet of the hotel room, I'd raise my arms and stomp about, like one of these dramatic dancers.

After Barcelona, we drove into the mountains to Madrid, via Segovia. My sister nearly swooned to be in the very location of Hemingway's *For Whom the Bell Tolls*. She and my mother spent a lot of time trying to pick out locations from the novel; in particular they grew misty-eyed when we stopped at a certain bridge where someone had died or been blown up or something. I yawned.

We spent the night in Segovia. As so often, I shared a room with Frances. She was terrified of spiders and disliked all insects, perhaps because they loved feeding on her. On our way to bed, my mother reminded us that scorpions were common in this part of Spain. Frances gave a little shriek and I shivered. I wasn't sure what a scorpion looked like, but I knew they had poisonous stingers. My mother often told a story of being in Mexico with my father and another couple after the war. In the shower, she'd glanced down to see a scorpion "waving its tail" at her from the drain at her feet. She yelped and dashed out of the shower *naked* into the living room. My father and his friend sprinted into the bathroom and stomped on the scorpion with their boots. Given that I'd never seen my mother undressed, I figured she must have been terrified to make such a spectacle of herself.

That night in Segovia, I awoke needing to pee. Not wanting to wake Frances, I made my way across the room to the bathroom in the dark, turning on the light only once I'd closed the door. Sitting on the toilet, half asleep, I saw a small scaly creature skitter across the floor and under the door into our room. Was it a scorpion? It looked nasty, but smaller than what I'd imagined from the shower story. My mouth went dry, but I didn't want to wake everyone and have them laugh at me for being afraid of a spider or something.

It might have been just a big spider. I sat there shivering for a while, then I turned off the bathroom light and made a mad dash back to my bed in the dark.

In the morning, I saw no sign of the creature. When I told Frances about it, she blanched, grabbed my arm and dragged me down the hall to my parents' room. My description convinced them that I had indeed seen a scorpion. My mother got that pinched look.

"What were you thinking?" my sister asked, her voice rising. "Scorpions are poisonous. You could have died!" She threw her arms around me and clutched me tight.

I shrugged. "Well, I didn't."

Despite this brave show, I didn't like to think what might have happened in the dark hotel room that night. When we began our return trip, I sighed in relief. Paris seemed safe and familiar compared to Spain. The only dangerous creatures I'd encounter there would be my classmates.

12

Turning the Tables

Returning to Paris felt like coming home. After incomprehensible Spanish, French seemed like my mother tongue. I could understand everything. My confidence soared and even the prospect of returning to school didn't bother me.

January in Paris felt mild compared to Canada. We never saw snow and although I missed it, at least the long walk to the new school didn't involve fighting our way through blizzards. I no longer walked with Baggasin on these treks; I managed to avoid her and link up with other girls. They ignored me but seemed less bothered by my presence than in the past. While I didn't speak, I understood every word spoken by my classmates and the forbidding *Madame la Maîtresse*.

Not long after the Christmas break, as we lined up at the end of the school day, Danielle asked me to walk with her. I stared at her, hardly able to believe my ears. She smiled warmly, and I nodded, thrilled. Although she'd never spoken to me before, I liked Danielle. She rarely joined the others in mocking me and seemed friendly and open. She took my arm and led me to the front of the line where Solange stood. My heart pounded with excitement. Perhaps my chance to be accepted by the elite had finally arrived. I felt like I'd been invited to court.

Solange, *la première dans la classe,* frowned. "What is this?" she asked Danielle. "I do not wish to walk with her."

So much for my dreams. I wanted to disappear into the earth, or at least back to my usual place near the rear of the line.

Danielle seemed unworried. "She is all right." She patted my arm encouragingly. "I thought it might make a change."

Solange tossed her dark blonde hair and winked at Danielle. "Very well. We can have some fun with her."

"Why not?" responded Danielle.

I didn't blame Danielle; Solange always called the shots. The other girls so desperately wanted to be her friends that they agreed to her every demand. Still, I'd been ridiculed during the walk home before, so I had a pretty good idea what "having some fun with her" meant.

"Let us pretend that Margarette is intelligent," giggled Solange.

Danielle nodded. I felt bereft.

"Perhaps this year you shall win the *prix d'or.*" Solange smiled sweetly at me. The gold prize was the most coveted award in the school; it went to the girl with the highest marks at the end of the year. No one doubted Solange would win it.

Solange turned to Danielle. "Does that not seem like a possibility to you? She has performed so well to date."

I stared at the ground. For a moment I'd thought Danielle really wanted to be my friend and that Solange might too. How could I be so foolish? Tears started to form in my eyes. Then I clenched my fists. This was my chance. If I let them taunt me now, I'd be scorned forever. Something steely grew inside me.

"Margarette," said Danielle, "what profession do you want to pursue when you grow up?" Did I detect a note of discomfort in her voice, possibly even sympathy?

"Oh, I expect she wants to be a doctor." Solange rolled her bright brown eyes and laughed.

"Actually," I said in perfect French, "I think I will become an actress. What do you plan to do?"

They gaped as though I'd told them I intended to be the Virgin Mary. I felt a rush of triumph.

They looked at each other. "She spoke," murmured Solange.

"Yes," I said. "I can speak. Does that surprise you?"

They looked so bewildered, I felt like laughing.

"Margarette," said Danielle in an urgent whisper. "You know how to speak French."

"Yes," I said in an offhand way.

"But you have never spoken before. We thought you were not capable of doing so."

"I know. But you were wrong, as you can see."

Solange's eyes grew enormous. "But this is *incroyable*," she whispered. "Astonishing. You have fooled us all!"

I smiled, almost beside myself with glee.

"Why have you kept this secret?" Solange asked, her low voice full of ... admiration.

Meg Westley

I lowered my voice to match theirs. It felt like a fabulous conspiracy, between me and the two shining stars of the class. "Well, at first I could not speak or understand, so I thought I would just wait until I could."

"She speaks perfectly," said Danielle.

"Oh, I think I might still make the odd mistake," I said.

"This is unbelievable," murmured Solange. "Tremendous." Their hostility and scorn had vanished. A few minutes ago, Solange had seemed patronizing. Now she seemed delighted and intrigued, as though I were the most spectacular creature she'd ever met. I felt light-headed.

"How did you spend your Christmas holidays?" Solange asked.

Wondering if this might be a test to see if I really could speak more than a few words, I proceeded to tell them about our trip to Spain. Their eyes widened even more.

"Flamenco dancers," murmured Danielle. "How I would love to see such a thing. What do they look like?"

"Very beautiful," I said, adopting the same quiet tone they both used, although not sure why our chat was so secretive. "They wear gorgeous dresses with big flounces on the skirts and they stamp their feet. I have a doll with a yellow dress and long black curly hair."

"A doll," breathed Solange.

We continued to talk in quiet voices. They told me about their holidays, aunts and uncles visiting, the presents they'd received. I could not quite believe I was having this conversation, as though we were old friends sharing secrets.

"This is so wonderful." Solange beamed at me. "You speak perfectly!" She looked over her shoulder. "No one else knows. Let us make them look like fools."

Danielle nodded, a wicked look in her eye.

I happily agreed to their plot. I'd been the butt of jokes since I arrived at the school, now it was someone else's turn. It never occurred to me to spare others what I'd been through. I think I'd have gone along with any suggestion of Solange's, so pleased was I to be breathing the rarified air around her. Besides, I wanted revenge.

Solange raised her voice. "Margarette, I think you are really rather clever."

The girls behind us tittered, their way of applauding Solange's wit.

"I agree," said Danielle, giving my arm a little squeeze. "It is so fascinating to hear about your adventures."

Adventures! Oh, I liked that; it made me sound so daring.

Laughter and whispers rippled along the line of girls as word of the "joke" being played out at the front passed back.

After a few more minutes of praise, which I did not mind at all, Solange turned to look at the girls behind her. "What is so amusing?" she snapped.

"Margarette! Clever!" Someone hooted and the laughter rose.

"Please, do not," said a soft voice. I glanced over my shoulder to see Sylvie watching me with an anxious look. My heart warmed to her more than ever; I felt a tiny bit guilty about tricking her.

Solange glared. "Yes, she is clever. You are just too stupid to realize it. She has travelled to Spain, you know, and she obtained a marvelous doll there. Is that not correct, Margarette?"

"Yes," I said, "a doll of a flamenco dancer. I will show it to you one day, Solange."

"That would be lovely," she said, sliding her arm through mine. "What else did you see there?"

"We drove right through the *Pyrénées* and saw the *Col de Ronceveaux.*" This wasn't precisely true, but I wanted to impress the crowd.

"The *Pyrénées!*" Danielle took my other arm.

Silence spread behind us.

"She speaks!" someone whispered.

Solange glanced back. "Of course, she speaks. Did you not realize?" She rolled her eyes.

A hubbub broke out all along the line as the word passed back. "The imbecile is not an imbecile at all." "Solange likes *la petite Anglaise!*" "Danielle is her friend!" "Who knew!" "Ooh la la."

Solange and Danielle grinned at me. I beamed, on top of the world.

When we parted ways to go home, Solange took my hands in hers and gazed at me seriously. "I am sorry I have not been very kind to you. I would like to be friends. Can we walk together again tomorrow?"

"That would be nice," I said, trying to contain my excitement. I raced home, delirious.

My mother stood in the kitchen chopping onions. She glanced up. "How was your day?" She gazed at me thoughtfully. "You look happy."

For a second I thought I'd just play it cool, but I couldn't. "I walked home with Solange! And Danielle! They want to be my friends!" I hurled myself onto the Louis Quinze sofa, ignoring the pain that shot through my elbow when it hit the carved wooden arm.

"Ah," said my mother, returning to her chopping. "I knew you'd make friends eventually."

It didn't even bother me that she was more or less saying *I told you so.*

The next day I arrived at school a little early, my stomach in knots. What if it had all been a ploy and nothing had really changed? I stood anxiously in the corner of the courtyard, waiting for Solange to arrive. Her mother brought her into the courtyard, as usual, kissed her on both cheeks and bustled away. I waited, pretending not to see her.

"Margarette!" she called.

I turned in her direction. She smiled and beckoned. Like a puppet on a string, I moved towards her, melting inside. We led the line to the new school together.

I became an overnight star, or at least an exotic new toy, although I preferred the star idea. Girls flocked to walk with me, to hear me talk, to ask me about *Angleterre.* They still did not understand that although I spoke English, I came from Canada. When I tried to explain this, their eyes glazed over. They knew nothing about Canada, but they knew about the treacherous English, long-time foes of the French. The two countries had fought for a hundred years! Now it seemed my "English" heritage gave me status. They had The Enemy in their midst and *ooh la la,* she spoke!

13

No Visitors Allowed

Having friends at school, and not just friends, but the *crème de la crème* of friends, transformed me. For months I'd been shy and uncertain, always worried about what people would think of me, trying not to attract attention. I'd struggled miserably with my schoolwork for the first time in my life. I had also been sickly, lacking energy and spunk. By early February, all that had changed.

While I did not like to admit it, the horse pills probably had something to do with my increased energy. I still loathed the hospital visits. Every month on the appointed day, my hands felt clammy. I knew the routine all too well. We'd drive to the medieval torture chamber they called a hospital. Doctors would examine me. Then the dreaded blood test. The medical staff knew me and anticipated my response. I didn't scream anymore but sometimes I threw up. According to my mother, I always turned green. They now put me on a cot to take blood so I could rest until my colour returned. The quantity of blood they extracted from my skinny arm never failed to frighten me. The bottle full of red liquid looked enormous. But apart from those miserable hospital visits, I felt pretty good.

At school I had begun to demonstrate that I was not, in fact, an imbecile. I amassed *Bon Points*, not just in arithmetic but in geography and history as well. I could write with the nib pen, flowing lines that made me proud. I won prizes in gym. I finally received my first *Petite Image*, then another and another. The girls rolled their eyes at first, as though it must be a fluke, but soon they began to look at me differently. I'm sure my rising academic star had something to do with Solange's change of attitude as well. (I mean, she'd never have befriended an idiot.) All in all, I felt reborn.

Although being Solange's closest friend remained my number one goal, I welcomed the attention of other girls as well and they embraced me now that Solange had bestowed favour upon me. In particular I was delighted to become friends with the beautiful Sylvie. A sweet gentle girl, she quickly reached out to me and I joined the throng admiring her rippling waist-length golden hair. Sometimes I had to give my head a shake when I received more walking invitations than I could accept. Mostly I gloried in the change and felt it was entirely my due.

I suspect I drove my parents crazy, even if they were pleased to see me restored to my old self. With my newfound confidence, I wanted to call the shots the way I used to in Montreal West. *Jeudis* had always been golden days, time to spend alone with my parents. Now I took no joy in such outings; I wanted to be with my friends.

"Solange," I said, one day as we dawdled in the courtyard during recess, feeling the warm sun on our faces, a hint of spring in the air already. "Would you like to come to my house to play on *jeudi*?"

She stared at me as though I'd lost my mind. "To your house? I do not think that would be possible."

Solange did not, after all, want to be my friend.

"Is something wrong?" She gazed at me with her clear brown eyes, her brow furrowed. Solange never missed a thing.

"No."

"Good then. Shall we tell stories?"

She did want to be my friend, but didn't want to play? It made no sense to me, but Solange distracted me with her stories. She read a lot and could spin a tall tale with finesse. In no time she had me enthralled with an account of a giant who ate little girls if they were not super polite to him.

A few days later, I tried Sylvie. "Would you like to come over to my house to play?"

"To play?" She smiled as though I'd told a joke.

"Yes, after school—or maybe on *jeudi*." I reached out to stroke her golden hair, a new privilege for me.

"Oh, I do not know. I have to do homework after school and help with the café." Sylvie's parents owned a café across the main boulevard from the school.

"But on *jeudi*?" I persisted.

"I do not think that would be possible." She smiled again.

When I got the same response from Danielle, I went home in a grump.

"No one wants to play with me," I mumbled.

My mother frowned. "I thought they liked you."

"Well I think they do, but they don't want to play."

"You don't play at school?" She looked bewildered.

I stamped my foot. "Of course, we play at school, but they don't want to come over." Parents could be so dense.

"Why not?"

"I don't know." I thought my life would change, but outside of school it remained the same.

"Why don't you ask?" said my ever-practical mother.

She didn't understand the delicacy of the situation. If I asked, I would surely be rejected outright. I didn't want to know that they didn't really want to spend time with me or that some French custom allowed children to consort with foreigners at school but nowhere else.

"I can't see why you wouldn't ask them." My mother, as usual, was cooking. Delicious aromas rose from the pan as she stirred. "Perhaps they've misunderstood. It would be silly to let a misunderstanding get in the way of your friendships."

"I don't think that's it," I said.

But her words stayed with me. I mulled on possible reasons for this distressing behaviour. Paying closer attention, I realized the girls' reluctance to come to my house did not seem to be directed at me personally. They didn't go to each other's houses either.

I decided Sylvie was least likely to make me feel like a fool, so the next time I found myself walking with her, I asked. "Sylvie, do you ever play with other girls outside of school?"

She considered and finally nodded. "Sometimes Marie comes to the café when her mother is working there, and we play."

I felt jealous. Sylvie had a friend named Marie I didn't even know.

"And when we visit the Bernards, I play with Elise, although she is younger, only six."

A suspicion grew in my mind. "But you never go by yourself to a friend's house?"

"Oh no." She gazed at me with round eyes, as though I'd suggested something improper.

I thought this over and later asked Solange the same question. Sure enough, it seemed that French children never visited each other's homes without their parents.

"How strange," I said. "At home, we visit each other all the time. Every day after school I go to a friend's house to play or have one over to my house."

Solange gave me an *Oh come on, you can't expect me to believe THAT* look.

"It is true!" I protested.

She gazed at me. "Every day? Truly?" Solange loved to hear about how I lived back in Montreal.

"Well, maybe not every day," I admitted. "But most days. We walk home from school together and go to one of our houses. And we play together until dinner time."

Her eyebrows rose as I spoke. "You walk home together, on your own, without your *maman*?"

I nodded. "I walk home by myself here in Paris too."

She looked away quickly. I felt uncomfortable, knowing that Solange's mother came every day to pick her up at school. Perhaps it embarrassed her. Or perhaps she thought it improper for me to walk alone.

"My *maman* would never allow it." She managed to sound defiant and wistful at the same time, which did nothing to clear up my confusion. "Look out!" She yanked me towards her so that I just avoided stepping in dog poop.

I yelped and we both laughed. The filthy state of Parisian streets never failed to shock me. Splatters from the *pissoires,* refuse, and dog droppings smeared the sooty black of the pavement. I preferred to look up, at the tall elegant buildings, but this had its dangers.

At home, I said to my mother. "There's something weird about France."

She laughed, her eyes crinkling up in a way I loved. "No kidding. What now?"

"Mothers don't let their kids play or walk alone or go to each other's houses. It's not me, it's the way they do things." I told her about my chat with Solange.

"Hmmm. They seem very protective. Maybe it's just that they don't know us and are worried about what we're really like. I could call her mother and introduce myself and invite her to bring Solange over."

"I don't know." What if that struck Solange's mother as too forward, pushy? I felt torn. My mother was very persuasive, but I hated the idea she might commit an inexcusable *faux pas*. Then Solange would never be allowed to come over.

My mother shrugged. "Well, I don't mind, if you want me to."

I hugged her, but dropped the topic, which obviously needed further research. Mom could be on the right track, but there might be more to this thorny matter. I had a mystery to solve: why did French mothers not allow their children to visit friends?

The next day I arrived at the old school early. My spirits lifted when Sylvie appeared by herself, no mother or other relative in sight. It made sense, for heaven's sake, she lived right across the street, but maybe it also meant her parents allowed her more freedom than the other girls'. I slipped into line next to her and as we trotted along to the new school,

I said, "Sylvie, do you think if my mother telephoned your mother to invite you to my house, you might be permitted to come?"

"Well." She gazed at me thoughtfully. "Perhaps. Your mother would really invite me to visit?" Her eyes lit up as though I'd suggested an exotic adventure.

"My mother would be happy to invite you," I said solemnly, once again puzzled by the oddness of the French. It had little to do with my mother. *I* wanted Sylvie to come play. But if my mother had to be involved, it could be arranged.

"Is it some kind of celebration?" She lowered her voice, so I barely caught her words.

"Ah…" I didn't know how to respond. Should it be a celebration? Was that what was required? No wonder visits were a rarity. "No," I said. "It would just be to play."

She looked bewildered.

"Sylvie, in my home country, people visit all the time. It is … a custom, a way to be friendly."

Sylvie clearly found this difficult to digest.

"Would it be better if it were a celebration? A party?"

She nodded vigorously. "Yes. A *fête* is different, something special, when you have a few dear friends to celebrate your birthday or something like that. I think my mother would accept such an invitation."

I felt tempted to ask more, to try to solve this Mystery, but I held back. It might not do to inquire too closely into their customs. It might seem like prying. We spoke of other things. I showed her my most recent *Petite Image*: a picture of a ballerina in pale pink, her arms spread and one leg lifted in an arabesque.

"She is very beautiful, is she not?" Sylvie sighed, gazing at the picture.

"Yes. Once I thought I might be a ballerina." The notion lingered still.

"Ah, yes. That would be wonderful, no?"

I raced home after school. Patrick and Josée sat on the curb, awaiting me.

"I'll be out later!" I called to them before dashing up the stairs. I had not spent much time with them of late, my mind filled with my new friends and the Mystery.

"Mom! I want to have a party!" I announced.

She looked up from her typewriter. "What for?"

"Because that's what they do here. They only go to each other's houses for parties!"

"That's ridiculous. You can't have parties all the time. What will the French think of next? Honestly."

"No, no, not all the time. Of course not. Just one party. Please, Mom?" I hadn't expected a negative response. I thought she was on my side.

"Hummph." She peered at the paper before her. She wrote articles about life in Paris that she sent home to be read on the radio. Hardly urgent, I thought.

"I mean, I didn't really have a birthday party. Couldn't it be a late birthday party?" On my birthday in December, my parents had taken Becky and me to see the movie *The Incredible Journey*, with French subtitles, of course. It had been a special event, but not a party.

"No. Don't be silly. It's way past your birthday." My mother could be a real stickler for detail.

"Okay, okay. Not a birthday party." Though disappointed after a brief vision of cake and presents, I didn't want to have a showdown about it. "How about … a Valentine's Party?" It was February after all.

My mother ran a hand through her hair and leaned back. "How many girls are you talking about?"

Aha! She was softening, I could tell. Of course, I wanted a big party, but I knew better than to push my luck. Besides I didn't really know that many girls. "Three or four?"

Finally, her face softened. "Well, I suppose you could have three friends over for a Valentine's lunch. Would that do?"

"Yes!!!" I hugged her and bounced around the room, singing, "I'm going to have a party!"

"Be careful of the furniture!"

"Sorry. Sorry." I perched on a chair, then jumped up again. "Oh, thank you, Mom!"

She sighed, but her eyes twinkled. I knew she was smiling inside. "These French and their protocols. Imagine, that you'd have to host a party to get friends to come over. It's a miracle they have friends at all. Maybe they don't. Maybe that's why they're so grumpy all the time."

I barely heard her. All I could think about was having Solange and Danielle and Sylvie over to play. I stared out at the View and dreamed about the party. Then a disturbing thought came to me. Did they even celebrate Valentine's Day in France?

14

Enchantée

The next day, I led Solange, Danielle and Sylvie to a private corner of the school courtyard.

"I am going to have a small party at my home and I am inviting all of you," I announced, watching them carefully.

"A party! How marvellous." Solange's eyes brightened. She glanced around the courtyard like a monarch surveying her realm.

Danielle looked uncertain. "Oh, I hope I will be allowed to come."

Sylvie smiled. "Very good, Margarette!"

"When will it be?" asked Solange.

"Next *jeudi*," I said, pleased with their response. "My mother will telephone your mothers, but you must give me the telephone numbers."

No problem. They all spewed out their phone numbers so quickly I had no chance of remembering them. I asked them to write their numbers down and give them to me.

"Will there be invitations?" asked Danielle.

I had not anticipated this. "Of course." I'd figure that out right after school.

"What will we be celebrating?" asked Sylvie.

"The Day of Saint Valentine!"

They glanced at each other, frowning a little. My heart sank. They didn't have Valentine's Day in Paris, just as they didn't have Halloween. Silly French. But I would not let this small detail interfere.

"It is a day when we celebrate love in Canada," I said.

Danielle blushed.

Sylvie said, "Ooh la la" in a slightly shocked tone.

"What do you mean?" demanded Solange.

I felt a little cross. What could possibly be wrong with a holiday celebrating love? "Saint Valentine was the saint of love. She had little cupids, babies with wings and silk scarves, who ran errands for her." I stumbled, having no very clear idea of the facts. But I had their full attention. "These little cupids shoot arrows. If one strikes you, you fall in love."

Solange sighed. "Ahhh."

"On the Day of Saint Valentine people give each other cards in the shape of hearts. And boxes of chocolates. It is very lovely."

My explanation sounded a bit lame. I didn't want to try to explain the jokes on the cards or the way sometimes people signed them "From Your Valentine." In fact, the more I thought about it, the less likely it seemed to me that anyone would ever throw a Valentine's Day party.

"We must make cards," Solange whispered to Danielle.

"I do not know if I will even be allowed to come." Danielle looked like she might burst into tears.

"Will we have chocolates?" asked Sylvie.

About to assure them we would have all the chocolate we could possibly eat, I realized I had not yet discussed any of the party details with my mother. "Yes, I am sure we will have chocolates. But you do not need to make cards."

"And games?" asked Solange. "Shall we shoot arrows at each other and swoon with love?"

Danielle and Sylvie giggled.

I loved Solange; she had the right spirit and imagination. "We can play whatever games we want."

We discussed possible games for the rest of recess. I had told them about seeing *West Side Story,* which was a truly tragic love story and we thought perhaps we could be Sharks and Jets, except they were boys, which wasn't appealing. Sylvie always wanted to play *La Belle et La Bête,* no doubt because she would be the obvious choice for La Belle.

At the end of the day I scampered home clutching the phone numbers. "We need invitations!" I announced to my mother.

"Why?"

I stroked her hand. "Because that is what they do here. They give out invitations."

She smothered a sigh. "Very well. You can make them."

I shuddered. I'd made invitations and cards before, but this was a terribly special occasion. What if the mothers refused to let the girls come because the invitations weren't nice enough? I opened my mouth to beg my mother to buy some. The steely look in her eye persuaded me to shut it again. "Okay. I'll make them."

I agonized. "What should they say?"

My mother, absorbed in peeling oranges, listed off the essentials: "Time, date, place, RSVP."

"But do you think they do it the same way here?" I so badly wanted to get this right.

"Does it matter? That's what they need to know. That's the information on all invitations."

It did matter, to me. I paced the Room With A View, trying to picture the perfect invitation. I considered asking for some money to go to the *librarie* to buy red paper so I could make heart-shaped cards. But maybe that would just look stupid. Then it came to me. "I'll ask Marie-Laurence! She'll know the proper way to write an invitation."

My mother sniffed. "Yes, I'm sure she would. Honestly, Meg, you're making an awful fuss about this. I'm beginning to wonder if it was a mistake agreeing to the party."

I turned my back on her and made a grand exit down the stairs. Then I raced into the courtyard behind our house. The vile stench almost made me gag. Did people actually pee back here instead of using toilets? I hurried across the courtyard and up the steps to Madame Wax's door. After catching my breath, I tapped politely.

Marie-Laurence opened the door. "*Bonjour, Margarette. Comment ça va?*"

"I am very well, thank you. Marie-Laurence, I need to make invitations for a party. Can you help me?" I had no time for small talk.

Madame Wax blossomed into view and enfolded me in her arms. "*Ah, la petite mignonne.* A party? How wonderful! What is the occasion?"

I gazed at Marie-Laurence desperately, fearful that I'd get trapped in time-consuming chitchat with Madame.

"Maman." Marie-Laurence hushed the flow of words from Madame. "I sense that Margarette has some urgency about this matter."

I nodded vigorously. Madame shrugged, kissed me and faded back to her corner of the room. Blessèd Marie-Laurence understood my challenge immediately. She produced lovely crisp stationary and showed me how to fold it to make little cards. Then she explained how to write a perfect invitation in French. The details did not differ much from what my mother had said, but Marie-Laurence knew the proper phrasing and way to express complex matters like the time. She lent me a lovely nib pen and I experimented to get all the curlicues correct. Dark had fallen as I showered Marie-Laurence with thanks for her assistance and beetled back across the courtyard.

I hurried upstairs and proudly displayed my invitations:

Cher Solange,

Vous êtes invitée à une petite fête chez moi!

Date: jeudi, le 13 fevrier
Heure: 13.00, pour dejéneur
Lieu: 6 rue Nicolet
R.S.V.P: 08 26 76 33 71

Margaret

"Lovely," said my mother. "Now sit down and eat."
I gobbled down my supper. "I need envelopes!"

My mother dug around in the desk drawers and produced some plain white envelopes. I slipped the invitations inside. "They're too big." The card looked lost inside the envelopes. My mother watched with a little smile. "Meg, if your friends don't want to come because the envelopes are too big, they aren't very good friends, are they?"

I was not convinced by this logic, but what could I do?

The next day I handed out the not-so-little envelopes. The girls seized them in delight, tearing them open and reading the invitations as though they might contain the word of God. Although they failed to comment on the *très belle écriture*, I felt very pleased.

Other girls gathered around asking, "What are those?"

Solange, ever the leader, announced, "Margarette is having a special party and we are invited."

The girls sighed and gazed at me with longing eyes.

"Can I come too?" asked one.

"No, I am so sorry. My *maman* said only three friends could attend." Inside I danced a little jig. Everyone wanted to come to *my* party.

My little *fête* became the talk of the schoolyard. Solange, Danielle and Sylvie chatted about what they would wear and what games we might play. They talked loudly about my flamenco dancer doll and how *they* would get to see it and hold it. Indeed, they did everything in their power to make the other girls jealous.

Two days later, I huddled in the Room With A View while my mother made the phone calls. We'd debated about whether she really needed to take this step, since I'd included the RSVP and our number on the invitations, but it seemed safest to go ahead. The mothers might be so hesitant that they would not even bother to call.

Despite my mother's sometimes painful pronunciation and occasional grammatical errors, the calls went well. Sylvie's mother said yes right away. Solange's mother needed more information and seemed a little uncertain, according to my mother, but she too agreed. The final call, to Danielle's mother, took the longest. My mother's face reddened as she spoke, and her voice got a little warning edge to it. I grimaced as she hung up.

"Well?" I asked.

"She wasn't very polite." My mother glared at the phone. "Acted as though I planned to kidnap her daughter. Really."

"But can Danielle come?"

"Yes. They can all come." She let out a great sigh and smiled at me. "I'm glad that's over with."

I gave her a big hug. "Thanks so much, Mom! Now, what will we eat at the party?"

I could talk of nothing else for the next week and badgered my poor mother relentlessly. I wanted chocolates, of course, for Valentine's Day and maybe a little heart-shaped cake?

"Not unless we can find one at the *pâtisserie*," said my mother firmly.

I agonized over what we should eat for the luncheon itself. What did little French girls eat at parties?

"What do *you* want to eat, Meg?" asked my mother.

"Macaroni and cheese!"

"Then that's what we'll have."

"But what if they don't like it?" The thought tortured me. I imagined them turning up their pretty noses or taking a single forkful and grimacing.

"Why wouldn't they like macaroni and cheese?" My mother's patience sounded like it was wearing thin.

"I don't know!"

"Meg, relax. You say your friends are excited to be coming over. We'll have chocolates and macaroni. The whole purpose of this is for you to have friends here to play with, right? You will have them. You can play. Now please, stop fussing."

I said no more. If she got really angry, she might cancel the party.

Finally, the great day arrived. I awoke far too early. Every hour I changed my clothes. We set the table three times. I gazed at the plate of chocolates, worried they might contain liquor despite the assurances of the *madame* at the *pâtisserie*. French people regarded liquor in chocolates as normal and might not have taken our urgent queries seriously. It never occurred to me that my friends might be accustomed to liquored chocolates.

When the doorbell tinkled at one o'clock, I almost fell down the stairs in my rush to respond.

"Slow down!" bellowed Mom.

"You'd better come down too," I called up.

"All right. I'm coming." I heard her stomping down as I threw open the door.

Sylvie stood there in a frilly blue dress, a large wrapped package in her hands. Her mother, a rosy-faced woman in a neat brown coat, said "Bonjour."

"*Maman*, this is Margarette." Sylvie beamed at me.

Her mother smiled. "*Enchantée, ma petite*."

My mother appeared and they exchanged greetings. I jumped in if my mother hesitated, anxious to impress, not wanting my mother to make any embarrassing mistakes. Sylvie's *maman* confirmed that she would return to pick up Sylvie at four o'clock, thanked my mother for inviting her and departed.

Sylvie presented the wrapped package to my mother. "Thank you very much for inviting me, Madame."

Having assumed the present was for me, I felt a little put out. My mother looked confused. The bell chimed again. I rushed to fling open the door.

Danielle and her mother faced me. I gabbled welcomes. Danielle wore a starched pink dress and held a basket in her hands. At an elbow jab from her mother, whose glum face looked more appropriate for a funeral than a party, Danielle handed the basket to my mother and mumbled her gratitude for the invitation. Her mother scowled and jabbed her again. Danielle repeated her obviously rehearsed little speech more loudly.

"Thank you very much," said Mom. "It is a pleasure to meet you, Danielle."

"*Enchantée, Madame,*" said Danielle.

I wanted to roll my eyes at how enchanted everyone seemed. Instead I stepped back from Danielle's formidable *maman* and whispered to the girls. "As soon as Solange arrives, we will have lunch!"

They seemed cowed by the presence of the mothers and gave me only the barest nods in response.

Danielle's mother proceeded to ask my mother what we would be doing and when she should return for Danielle, her tone frosty.

I leapt in to explain, fearful of my mother's French. "We will have our luncheon and then play some games—" I faltered as Danielle's mother glared at me.

"Take your friends upstairs," murmured my mother.

Not wanting to remain in the company of Danielle's mother, I turned to the girls. "Follow me. I will show you our *salon.*"

We'd barely reached the Room With A View when the doorbell rang again. "Take a seat. I will return promptly," I said and bounced down the stairs again, almost crashing into my mother.

Solange too held a parcel; she wore a white and gold dress with a big sash. Her mother, a small, pale woman, smiled at me timidly and interrupted my eager introductions and explanations.

"Madame," she said to my mother. "May we have a word?"

"But of course," Mom responded. In English she said, "Run along now, Meg."

Solange, grinning broadly, gave her the parcel and the two of us raced up the stairs.

Danielle and Sylvie perched on the Louis XV sofa. For a few minutes we engaged in uncomfortable chitchat, almost like grown-ups. Then I produced my flamenco dancer doll. They gazed at her in awe, then each wanted to hold her. By the time my mother returned, we were all prancing around, snapping our fingers, and tossing our heads Spanish-style. I noticed my mother quietly removing all the forks from the table. She replaced them with spoons, which struck me as odd since we'd be eating macaroni.

When we sat down to eat, the girls looked at the macaroni with doubt. I feared they thought it somehow inappropriate fare, but after a minute, they picked up their spoons.

"Why spoons, Mom?" I asked in English.

"I'll tell you later," she murmured.

The girls loved the creamy macaroni and cheese. They also enjoyed the chocolates, which did *not* contain liquor. We all behaved like little ladies at the luncheon table, except when we burst out giggling. Then we played *La Belle et la Bête* for Sylvie, taking turns being ferocious beasts. We danced *Swan Lake*, without any music, and we made Valentine's cards for each other. I told them exactly what to do and Mom supplied the red paper. We would have played tag, but my mother forbade it because of the furniture.

"We could go outside," I said in English.

"No," my mother said with unexpected force. "Not outside. Just play in here."

Under ordinary circumstances I'd have argued, but something in her voice told me it would be pointless. We abandoned the idea of tag and crawled around pretending to be animals, making most unladylike noises and laughing ourselves giddy.

When the mothers arrived at precisely four o'clock, I didn't want my friends to leave. But the girls trooped down obediently. The mothers expressed their gratitude and the daughters echoed them, all prim and proper. My mother thanked them again for the gifts. Each of the girls kissed me on both cheeks and they all departed.

My mother heaved a sigh. "Well. Did you have fun?"

"Oh yes. It was fantastic."

"They are very polite little girls," she said.

We climbed the stairs and she proceeded to open the packages. The basket contained fruit and *petit biscuits*, Sylvie's package a huge jar of wrapped *bonbons* and the parcel from Solange a lovely glass bowl.

"My goodness," said Mom. "This seems excessive. I mean it was just lunch."

I extracted a *bonbon* and popped it in my mouth.

"They're terribly formal, aren't they?" she said.

I nodded, happily sucking on the lemon-flavoured candy.

"I had an interesting chat with Solange's mother." She began to tidy up.

"Oh?" They had been downstairs for a while.

"Apparently Solange is not very good at using a knife and fork. That's why I put out spoons."

I stared at her. "Really?" I couldn't believe the ever-accomplished Solange wouldn't know how to eat properly.

"Yes, I thought it was bizarre. Maybe that's why they don't allow visiting. They don't want their children's lack of table manners to embarrass them." She shrugged. "Solange's mother worries about her."

"Really?" I said again. What could her mother possibly have to worry about? Solange was the *première dans la classe* and the most confident girl I'd ever met.

"Yes," she said. "That's why I wouldn't let you play outside. Solange's—" She paused.

"What?"

She smiled and shook her head. "Nothing. I'm glad you had fun, Meg. They seem like lovely girls. Good friends for you."

Yes, I thought, *they're my friends!* I crunched my candy happily.

15

Sylvie's Café

My little *fête* made me famous at school. Solange, Sylvie, and Danielle talked about it nonstop for the next two days, describing my doll, the chocolates, and the Valentine's cards we'd made. I could hardly believe everyone thought it such a big deal. Suddenly I was not just *la petite Anglaise,* but a girl who hosted parties, a seemingly unique creature. My classmates now looked at me with respect and even longing. They clustered around, eager for my attention, perhaps hoping I would invite them to my next *fête.*

Confident now, I worked harder at school and began to experience real success. On one history assignment I got the top mark in the class, beating even Solange. Madame did not smile, of course, but she did say *"Très bien, Margarette"* as she handed back the paper. I knew by now that this was very high praise. Solange looked surprised and I feared she might be annoyed. Then she grinned and gave me a little wink. I think she considered me her *protégé* and took pride in my achievement.

At home, everyone applauded my Parisian accent and fluency in French. I could hardly remember struggling with the language. French seemed so easy to me; I couldn't understand why my siblings and parents still had trouble with pronunciation, cadence or grammar. On outings I became the family spokesperson, chattering away to *Madame ou Monsieur*. I even dreamt in French.

Solange and I ruled the schoolyard, deciding what games to play and who to include. Solange did not favour Sylvie as much as I did, although I couldn't figure out why. I adored Sylvie. When I asked Solange about it, she said, "Of course I like Sylvie. She is very pretty," and dropped the subject. But she did not always include Sylvie in our games. On the other hand, she almost invariably invited Danielle to join us. I didn't really care who she invited as long as she wanted me involved and she always did. I wondered if Danielle might resent me. She and Solange had been the very best of friends until I came along. Once I heard Solange whisper to Danielle about Sylvie, "Well, her *maman et papa* work in the restaurant, don't they?" Both of them giggled. I didn't see the humour, but sometimes I just did not get my friends' jokes.

Sylvie did not seem bothered by the occasional exclusion. She would shrug and smile and move off with her followers. Sylvie always had girls eager to spend time with her and she just did not seem to care about being with the *crème de la crème*. I found her attitude endearing, even if I did not share it. I never wanted to be excluded again.

Baggasin had faded into the background. Every now and again I would see her watching me. When our gazes met, she would smile and if no one was looking, I'd nod; her grin would broaden as though I'd given her a present. I felt a combination of guilt and irritation. She had been kind to me when I was no one and for that I owed her gratitude at least. But her filthy smock, runny nose, and vacant expression offended me. I wondered how I could have befriended her and felt somewhat ashamed that I had. Certainly, I didn't want any of my new friends to think I cared about her at all, so I avoided her. Sadly, she seemed to expect and understand this.

Two weeks after my party, Sylvie's mother called mine. I hovered, trying to decipher the conversation based on my mother's side of it.

"Oh, it is not anything," said Mom. "Your daughter was behaving very well. It was our pleasure ... Well, yes, I think that yes ... On Thursday?" She frowned as though trying to remember.

"What?" I whispered, beside myself with curiosity.

She shook her head at me and spoke into the receiver. "May I return your telephone? I should consult."

I grimaced at her ineptitude and wished I could wrench the phone from her hand and speak to Sylvie's *maman* myself.

"Good-bye. It has been so pleasant. I will return your telephoning right away... yes. Good-bye."

"What? What did she want?"

My mother grinned at me and leaned back in her chair. She looked the way I imagined the canary-eating cat might. Not that we used such a term in our house. A cat once ate my sister's budgie and she cried for days.

"What?" I could hardly contain myself.

"Sylvie's mother wonders if you would like to go to their house to play on Thursday."

"Really?" I leapt to my feet and twirled about. "Can I? Can I?"

She laughed. "Of course you can."

After she had returned the call and confirmed that I should go there for the afternoon, she said, "I suppose you'd better take some sort of gift. It seems to be the thing to do."

I nodded, grateful that she'd remembered this custom.

"I understand they live above their restaurant."

"Neat." I could hardly wait to see the place.

The next day Sylvie spoke to me as we were lining up for the walk to the new school. "So, you will come to visit on *jeudi*?"

"Yes, yes! I look forward to it very much." I grinned at her.

Solange gave me an odd look. "You will go to Sylvie's, at the café?"

Sylvie and I nodded.

Solange raised her eyebrows slightly and turned to talk to Danielle. Jealous, I figured. To be honest, I'd have preferred to go to Solange's, but she had not invited me.

My mother fussed about what kind of gift I should take, grumbling. "It's all so silly. Suppose it becomes a regular thing, you playing with Sylvie. Will we have to buy presents every time you drop in? Will she keep bringing presents? The house will be stuffed with candy!"

I didn't think that sounded so bad and really had no answer to her question, but I agreed that I'd better bring something along in return for the gift Sylvie had brought.

On *jeudi* I was prepared to walk to Sylvie's on my own. The café nestled on the corner across the street from the old school I walked to every day.

"I think I'd better come along," said Mom. "They might think it funny if I didn't. You know, when in Rome..."

"But we're not in Rome, we're in Paris!"

She grunted. "It's an expression."

We set off, following the route I took every day. To get to school I only had to cross the small street of shops at the bottom of *rue Nicolet*. To reach the café, we had to cross the major intersection of *rue Custine* and *rue de Clignancourt*. We waited for the lights to change. Mad Parisian drivers careened past, honking their horns and swerving around parked cars. As we started across, Mom seized my hand. I tried to shake it off, not wanting to be treated like a little girl. She clung firm.

"Mom!"

"It's dangerous." She did not release me until we'd reached the sidewalk. Then she handed me the fancy bag of *bonbons* she'd purchased at the *pâtisserie*. "Now, be polite."

The nerve. As though I didn't know more about Parisian manners than she did.

We entered the café. Loud chatter and the clink of cutlery and glasses filled the long room. I peered around for Sylvie, feeling uncomfortable in this big crowded place. I spotted her at the far side of the café and waved. She said something to one of the waiters and skipped over to me.

"*Bonjour Madame. Bonjour Margarette.*" She kissed me on both cheeks.

A moment later, her mother appeared, red-faced. She beamed at us, kissed my mother on both cheeks and then me. I handed her the bag of *bonbons*.

"Oh, this is not necessary at all." She smiled, tucking a damp curl behind her ear. "But very kind of you." She turned to my mother. "It is all right with you if they play upstairs? We are working, you see."

"Of course." My mother looked a little bewildered. "What time would you like me to collect her?"

"Oh, whenever you like," said Sylvie's *maman*. "They can play and have a small snack."

"Very good. Shall I come for her around five o'clock? Is that too late?"

"No, that is perfect. Whenever you like. I will be here."

I could see my mother struggling with how informal this all seemed compared to the way everyone behaved at our house, but she nodded and said, "Five o'clock then. Thank you so much for having Meg ... er ... Margarette to play."

"It is nothing. Our pleasure." She shouted over the din of the restaurant.

"Very well. Good-bye, Madame. Until five o'clock," said Mom. "Behave yourself," she said to me in English. "And have fun."

"I will! Bye!"

Mom left and Sylvie's mother bustled back to the bar. Sylvie grabbed me by the hand and led me through the tables. "François is making a cake. Shall we watch?"

I had not expected anything like this. "If you like."

She pushed open a door at the far end of the restaurant and we entered the kitchen. I looked around at the stainless-steel counters, piles of clean dishes, pots steaming on stoves. A man with short dark hair and thick eyebrows stirred a huge bowl of batter, another had his arms up to the elbows in a sink of soapy water. A woman rushed past with two plates of salad. I felt both fascinated and intimidated by this strange environment.

Sylvie pulled up a stool by the dark-haired man and told me to sit. She then clambered up onto the edge of the counter. "François, this is my friend Margarette."

He glanced at me with smiling black eyes. "*Enchanté, ma petite.*"

I murmured, "*Moi aussi.*"

"Tell us what you are making," said Sylvie.

"This is a hazelnut torte." He whipped the large spoon around the batter. It smelled delicious, rich and sweet. "I will form it into layers with hazelnuts and cream in between and then top it in chocolate."

"Ahh," said Sylvie and I in one breath.

Waiters and Sylvie's *maman* rushed back and forth between the kitchen and the restaurant carrying plates and trays with coffee in bowls or tiny cups. People shouted out orders and practically crashed into each other, yet nothing fell to the floor. The air was thick with the rich smells of cooking.

We watched François pour the batter into shallow pans and pop them in a huge black oven. Then he chopped hazelnuts with a fast-flashing knife and stirred liquid chocolate on the stove. It smelled heavenly. When the cakes were baked, he let them cool while he whipped cream into caps with a whisk. I couldn't believe how fast he moved the whisk. My mother used electric beaters. Finally, he assembled the torte, spreading layers of hazelnut and cream between the thin cakes, drizzling chocolate over the top, and finishing it off with a delicate dusting of sugar.

"*C'est trés beau,*" said Sylvie, jumping down.

"*Oui, c'est magnifique,*" I breathed.

He smiled and turned away.

"Shall we go upstairs?" asked Sylvie.

I gazed longingly at the torte, but apparently we would not get a taste; it was for the restaurant customers. Besides, I wanted to play! I followed Sylvie through the kitchen, dodging waiters, and through another door that led to a set of narrow wooden stairs. She pushed a switch on the wall and a bare bulb lit the stairway. The switch kept clicking as we climbed.

"What is that noise?" I asked.

She looked at me blankly. I pointed back at the switch.

"It is a timer. The light will stay on for half a minute, then go off."

Sure enough, we were plunged into darkness just as we reached the top of the steps. Sylvie opened the door into a narrow corridor. "This is where we live," she said. I trailed after her as she gave me a tour. There were only four rooms: her parents' bedroom, the room she shared with her older sister, a tiny bathroom that did not smell very fresh, and a living room with a couch, a chair, and a TV. All the rooms were small and dark, with windows facing exterior walls. Lacy covers did little to conceal the worn quality of the furniture. In comparison, *6 rue Nicolet* looked like a mansion.

"Where is the kitchen?" I asked.

She laughed aloud. "We were just there!"

"But ... but that is the restaurant kitchen. You do not have one up here?"

"No. We do not need one. We eat downstairs."

"You eat all your meals in the restaurant?" That sounded like luxury to me.

"Yes, of course. My *maman* and *papa* are always working, and I help sometimes too, clearing the tables and putting out the bread. So, it is most convenient to eat there. We will have a snack there later, when it is not so full."

I liked this idea immensely: eating our snack at a café table. It sounded very stylish. Perhaps we'd get a slice of the torte after all.

We spent the whole afternoon upstairs on our own. None of Sylvie's family ever came up. I could not recall ever being in a house without parents around. In Montreal West, children my age were never left alone. It seemed somehow inappropriate that Sylvie and I should have such independence. True, both her parents were close by, but they had no idea of our whereabouts or actions. We could do whatever we wanted, and no one would know.

In her room, Sylvie showed me her dolls. She had one made of porcelain, quite old-fashioned, that I thought very beautiful. We played hide and seek, or *cache cache*, after some debate about the rules. The dim, quiet rooms reminded me of the attic of an old farmhouse I'd visited in Quebec: everything was rough and dark and had a faint musty smell. I thought of the house full of secrets in *The Lion, The Witch and the Wardrobe* and told Sylvie the story as we sat on the balcony with our feet dangling, watching the courtyard life. I combed Sylvie's lovely hair and we dressed up in her sister's clothes.

At four o'clock, Sylvie said, "Let us go and have our snack."

We tumbled down the narrow staircase. The kitchen, much quieter now, seemed enormous compared to the rooms upstairs. Sylvie introduced me to her *Papa*, a round gentleman with piercing blue eyes. He said hello, ruffled Sylvie's hair and turned away to shout at one of the kitchen staff. Sylvie's *maman* came in, all smiles. "You are enjoying yourselves, my girls?"

"*Oui, Maman.*"

"Yes, very much. Thank you," I said.

"But now perhaps you are a little hungry?"

We both nodded. I couldn't see the torte anywhere.

"*Bien.* Why do you not run over to the *boulangerie* and buy two fresh croissants and I will make you some hot chocolate. Would you like that?"

"Oh yes," said Sylvie, as though this were a major treat.

Her mother gave her a few centimes and we trotted out into the busy street.

"Do you always buy croissants at the *boulangerie*?" I asked.

"But of course. Where else would we buy them?" Sylvie looked astonished.

"Well, I thought perhaps you made them in the restaurant."

"No, no, no. We buy bread for the restaurant at the *boulangerie*. And croissants in the morning for our patrons. But it is a special treat to have a croissant for afternoon snack. It is because you are here." She grinned and took my hand.

We skipped down five doors to a busy *boulangerie*, larger than the one near our house. The *madame* greeted Sylvie with a smile and raised her eyebrows when Sylvie asked for two croissants.

"For me and my friend Margarette," she explained. "She is my guest this afternoon."

"Ah," said Madame. "A special day!" She placed two croissants in a thin paper bag and gave them to Sylvie, who handed over her coins.

Back at the café, Sylvie's mother indicated a table by the window where two huge bowls steamed. We sat down.

A rich chocolate aroma arose from the bowls topped with mounds of whipped cream. We tore the croissants into pieces, dipped them in the chocolate and rolled our eyes in pleasure as we ate them. It all felt terribly grown-up: sitting at our own table in the café, gazing out at the people hurrying along the *rue*. When my mother appeared, I felt shocked. Surely the afternoon could not be at an end already!

She entered and smiled to see us at the table sipping from our bowls. Sylvie's *maman* reappeared and asked if she would care for a little *apéritif*. My mother shook her head, thanked her, and said we had to leave.

"I hope Meg behaved well," she said.

"Oh yes," said Sylvie's mother, although she'd hardly seen me all afternoon.

"Perhaps next week, Sylvie could come and play at our house again," said my fantastic mother.

To my surprise, Sylvie's mother nodded, as though this were a perfectly normal suggestion. "If it would not be too much trouble for you."

"No trouble at all. But she must not bring any more gifts. It is enough pleasure to have her visit."

"Very well," said Sylvie's *maman*.

After another round of cheek-kissing and thanks, we departed.

"Well, I think we've finally broken the social ice," said my mother.

16

Social Butterfly

The day after my visit to the café, Solange did an odd thing. Normally on our hike from the old school to the new, she walked in the middle of the first threesome in the line. This morning, she took the outside right position and manoeuvred me into the middle, with Danielle on my left. Ignoring Danielle, Solange slipped her arm through mine and proceeded to whisper to me.

"So, how was your visit to Sylvie's home?"

"Fine. We played and ate our snack in the café. Fresh croissants and hot chocolate."

"Hmmm. Yes. And what was her home like?" Solange breathed into my ear, as though we were conspiring in some way.

"Interesting. They live above the restaurant."

"Ah," she said knowingly. "Just rooms upstairs?"

"Yes." I did not care for her tone.

"And tell me about her parents. Were they there?"

"Of course. In the café. They were working, so we had no one to bother us at all. It was lovely."

She sniffed.

"Her mother is very kind and pleasant," I said. "We spent some time in the restaurant kitchen watching one of the chefs make a torte and we sat at a table in the window to eat our snack, just like grown-ups."

"I am sure it was very lovely, Margarette." Her tone suggested she doubted it could possibly have been lovely.

I didn't want to fight with Solange, but I felt a little cross. She seemed to be suggesting that Sylvie's home or family were in some way inferior. So, I refrained from saying anything about the lack of kitchen upstairs or the small dark rooms. Instead I said, "Yes. And I think Sylvie will come to play at my house next week. My mother invited her."

"Just Sylvie?" she asked in a small voice.

I nodded. She looked hurt. I felt a little badly, but after all she had not invited me to her house; Sylvie had.

"Since Sylvie invited me to play," I added quickly, "I think my mother wanted to return the favour. But I am sure I will be able to have you to play another time."

Solange said little the rest of the way to school, so I chatted with Danielle about homework. We had a geography test that day, so we quizzed each other. There'd been a great deal of information to memorize. We parroted back all kinds of facts to Madame every day. This time we'd have to write them all down, but I no longer felt panicky about either the memorization or the writing. I hoped to do well on the test and get the *Bon Point* I needed for another *Petite Image*.

As we talked, I watched Solange out of the corner of my eye. She seemed deep in thought; I'd seen the same expression as she plotted a ruse. As we arrived at the new school, her brow smoothed. She squeezed my arm. "I would like you to come and see my house."

I grinned. "I would like that very much too."

"I will speak to my *maman*." She smiled. "I think she will agree."

My heart pounded. Knowing Solange, I felt certain her mother would indeed agree. I liked Sylvie very much and did not like Solange's implied criticisms of her, but I was thrilled at the thought of being invited to Solange's. Then we would surely be best friends.

Distracted, I made a mistake on my test. Of course, Solange produced a flawless one, but this did not irk me. She sat close to me and we whispered as we worked on an embroidery project. A month earlier, Madame had given us each a square of yellow fabric with a wide weave, some thick blue thread, and a needle. She then directed us to use a particular stitch all around the outside edge of the square. If we made a mistake, we had to pluck out the offending stitches and start again. We'd been working on this maddening embroidery for some time and I'd unstitched as much as I'd stitched. The stitching became more complicated with each row of border. In the end, Madame had informed us firmly, it would be a beautiful item, of what use I could not imagine. Solange's looked quite pretty, and I wanted mine to be nice too, but embroidery, it seemed, was not my forte. I groaned as my needle stabbed through the wrong bit of the fabric.

"Do not worry," said Solange under her breath. "This is mere manual work. It has nothing to do with intelligence, whatever Madame may say." She rolled her eyes and we both giggled. Madame glanced our way but did not rebuke us.

Only Solange could get away with giggling in class and I now sat within the circle of her protection.

Days passed and Solange did not mention the potential visit to her house again. I grew anxious, fearful that her mother would somehow withstand Solange's pleas. Or that she might think me an unworthy guest. I still couldn't fully grasp the subtleties of Parisian society. Baggasin stood at the bottom of the ladder; no girl in my class would ever invite her to play and I could understand. Her slovenly ways were off-putting. Sylvie, although clearly more acceptable than Baggasin, also seemed tainted, at least in Solange's view, by the fact that her parents owned a café, or worked in it, or lived above it. This bewildered me. Who cared what someone's parents did? Sylvie was pretty and engaging and kind, her parents polite and friendly. Yet, I never questioned Solange's views.

The day before Sylvie's visit to my house, Solange did not seek me out as a walking companion, so I stepped into line next to Sylvie and we chatted about what we would do the next day. My mother had recently taken me to a French library, and I'd signed out a book of fairy tales. I promised Sylvie we could read them and maybe enact some of the stories. Solange glanced back at us, frowning.

That *jeudi*, Sylvie spent the afternoon at our house. My mother had suggested she come for lunch, but Sylvie's *maman* said it would be more convenient if Sylvie came a little later.

"I got the impression she felt it would be an imposition if Sylvie ate lunch here," said my mother. "As though I'd go to any trouble."

My father the sociologist had become quite interested in my excursions into Parisian society. "Perhaps it is not the norm here for children to visit for meals. It may be that the French regard meals as sacred family time, which Sylvie would interrupt if she came for lunch. What do you think, Meg?"

"I don't know." The question felt prying, but my father looked so keen to know my thoughts that I added, "Maybe. Or maybe they need Sylvie to help in the café at lunchtime. I didn't get the impression that they ate a lot of family meals together. They work all the time."

"Interesting. How old is Sylvie?"

"I think she's eight." I had turned nine in December.

"Hmmm. Is it usual for children that young to work in Paris?"

"Bill," said my mother. "It's a family business. Not like they're sending her out to work."

I nodded. "She just helps out." But I wondered about this. I could not imagine Solange working. It would be beneath her.

"But obviously they are working class," said my dad.

"And maybe they don't have much money," said my mother. "So, it would strain their resources to have an additional mouth to feed and they're just being considerate of us."

I thought about the croissants we'd bought for our snack and suddenly felt guilty. Sylvie had called it a special treat. I hoped it didn't mean they'd gone hungry later. But this hardly made sense. Sylvie was plump; she couldn't be starving.

This time Sylvie brought only a small bag of fragrant cookies. "François made them!" she announced.

My mother thanked her and said to her *maman*, "This is very kind of you, but not needed. We are happy to have Sylvie to entertain Meg."

Sylvie's *maman* smiled. "Oh, it is nothing. He made them for the restaurant anyway. Just a small treat for the girls." Then she turned to leave. "I must get back to the café, you know."

When we went to the upper room to play, Sylvie was quiet and very polite. Figuring my parents' presence might be making her nervous, I suggested we go down to my room. She seemed relieved. We bounced on the bed until my mother shouted at me to stop. Then I read the story *Les Fées* aloud from my borrowed book. Sylvie lay on the bed, looking like Rapunzel with her rippling gold hair spread over the pillow. She didn't move through the whole story except to sigh when diamonds and pearls fell from the lips of the unloved sister and gasp when the other sister spat out toads and vipers. I felt very pleased with my reading skills.

Next we had to enact the story. Naturally Sylvie played the kind beautiful sister while I crouched over like the fairy disguised as an old hag. Then I got to make disgusting noises and shriek my head off as I pretended to spit out snakes and toads. Sylvie laughed so hard she could hardly speak.

We had some of her cookies for a snack and my mother let us drink Fanta. I didn't feel so sad when she left this time. Our time together had seemed more natural and relaxed, no big deal, much more like playing with a friend at home.

That evening the telephone rang. My mother answered it and, after a moment, responded in French. "Yes, *Bonsoir Madame* ... Yes, yes ..." She winked at me.

I bounced over to her side.

"Oh I am sure Margarette would be very pleased … This Sunday? Are you sure? … At what hour?" She jotted down *Solange—5:00.*

I twirled about in glee. At last!

"For dinner?" My mother sounded astonished. "Are you sure? We would not want to inconvenience you—Well, if that suits you, yes I believe she could stay."

Dinner! I felt a little awed, even nervous. This was clearly a very special invitation.

After writing down the address on *rue Custine,* my mother repeated her thanks and hung up, smiling broadly.

I threw myself into her arms. "That was Solange's mother? Really?"

She hugged me. "Yes, it was. And they want you to come for dinner. Ooh la la!" She laughed. "You are becoming quite the social butterfly."

"At last! I'm going to Solange's!" I sang out.

"It sounded like this would be a family dinner, so you must behave well."

I danced around the room. "Oh, I will! I will!"

"At least you know how to use a knife and fork," she said under her breath.

Yes, I thought proudly. My mother would not have to tell Solange's to set out spoons, although I still could not imagine Solange struggling with a knife and fork. Perhaps there was one thing I could do better than Solange, but at that moment I didn't care. I just knew that I had been invited to her house for dinner. Not Danielle, not anyone else but me. And not just to play, but for dinner!

"Honey, there's something I think you should know before you go there." My mom beckoned me over to sit beside her on Louis's couch.

"What?" Her serious tone made me wary.

"You know how Solange's mother seems so protective of her?"

"Uh huh."

"Well, she told me that Solange had an older brother who was hit by a car crossing *rue Custine.*"

"Oh no." I thought of the cars revving their engines at the intersection and racing along the boulevard. Once, in Montreal West I'd run across our street without looking because I was late for school and a car had nicked my elbow. It scared me senseless. The driver screeched to a stop, and leapt out, his face scrunched in concern. I told him I was fine; the elbow didn't even hurt. He'd wanted to drive me to school but I knew better than to get into cars with strangers, even if they seemed nice.

"What happened?" I asked my mom.

Her eyes grew sad. "He was killed."

I blinked back tears. Poor Solange. I tried to imagine how I'd feel if Frances or Neil were killed by a car. I couldn't bear the thought.

Mom put an arm around me and pulled me close. "It was several years ago, I think. I didn't mean to upset you, but I thought you should know so you don't ask any awkward questions about her family."

I nodded. My mother was very wise. It would have been awful if I raised a topic that could make everyone sad.

That night I dreamt that I asked Solange about her brother. She burst into tears and her mother banished me from their house forever.

17

Dîner Chez Solange

Sunday dawned bright and sunny. Spring breezes ruffled the leaves on the trees and the air seemed light. Around three o'clock, I donned my blue summer dress with the wide white collar. My mother polished my black patent leather shoes with Vaseline and brushed my hair.

I'd quizzed Solange about what to expect at dinner.

"It will be family," she said, her eyes alight with excitement. "For Sunday dinner. My mother will cook a fine meal."

"Who will be there?" I wanted to know. Family could mean anything, as could "a fine meal."

"Oh, my parents, my aunt and uncle, my cousins, and my grandmother."

The thought of this crowd gathering to judge me made my stomach wobble.

Solange squeezed my hand. "They all want to meet you. I have told them so much about my good friend, the English girl."

I'd swallowed and nodded, reassured. She seemed as excited as I felt, but I doubted she shared my anxiety.

Dressed and brushed, I wandered restlessly about the house. My brother had gone out somewhere. My sister sat at the table in the Room With A View doing homework. She studied a lot, determined to be top of her class—a goal she regularly achieved. She glanced up.

"You look great, Meg. Excited?"

I nodded.

She leaned back. "You like Solange a lot, don't you?"

I nodded again.

"Tell me about her."

"Well …" How to describe Solange? "She's the smartest girl in the class, by far, and tons of fun. Likes playing pranks and games. All the other girls are crazy about her."

"It's great you've made such a good friend." She smiled at me. "And you've learned to speak French so well. I know it wasn't easy, but you stuck with it. I'm proud of you, Meggie."

I hugged her. I could always trust Frances to boost my confidence when I was feeling uncertain.

My mother looked up from her book and smiled. "Well, I guess you're all set. We'll leave in ten minutes, okay?"

I nodded, but it seemed like forever to me. I fingered the wrapping on the gift we'd bought, a fancy little ceramic bowl filled with handmade chocolates. I kept thinking about Solange's brother and wondering if the whole family would be sad. Dinner might be a gloomy affair.

By the time we left, I'd pushed thoughts of nasty car accidents to the back of my mind, but I did not object when Mom took my hand to cross *rue Custine*.

We reached *numero 12*, a tall stone building. My mother examined the names on the buzzers and pressed one. The tall door with a handle in the middle clicked loudly. We made our way into the dark foyer, found the light switch, and climbed the stairs, hitting another switch when we reached the landing. At the second floor, before my mother could knock on the door marked 5, it opened, and Solange stood there beaming. I forgot about her brother and kissed her on both cheeks. She grabbed my hand and pulled me into the apartment, calling, "*Maman*, Margarette has arrived!"

Her mother hurried to greet mine. They exchanged pleasantries and discussed the pick-up time. My mother suggested seven o'clock.

"*Mais non*," said Solange's mother anxiously. "Better eight-thirty or nine. We will not be finished *dîner* before then. If that is all right."

I knew Mom would think that was late, on a school night, but she merely nodded and thanked Madame. Giving me a little wink, she left.

I was alone, at Solange's. I presented the gift to Solange's *maman*. "Thank you so much for inviting me. It is very kind of you, Madame."

She took it with a smile. "You are most welcome, Margarette. It is our pleasure to have you here. Now I must return to the kitchen. Solange will entertain you."

She headed off down a hallway from which tempting smells wafted.

"Come," said Solange, "I will show you our home."

The apartment featured high ceilings and windows that looked out onto *rue Custine*. I had a brief vision of Solange's mother looking down and seeing the accident. Banishing it, I followed Solange into a large comfortable living room, where a man with a thin moustache and greying blond hair sat reading a newspaper. He glanced up at us blankly. I knew the look; my father had the same expression when his thoughts were elsewhere. Then he peered at me.

"And you are Solange's little English friend, yes?" He rose and extended his hand to me. I shook it.

"Yes, Papa, this is Margarette."

"*Enchanté, Mademoiselle,*" he said with a serious little half bow.

I made a sort of curtsey, at which Solange laughed. What was I thinking?

He settled back on the couch. "So, tell me, where are you from?"

"Canada," I responded. "Montréal."

He raised his eyebrows. "Ah, across the ocean then. That must have been a long journey."

Despite his serious manner, I liked him. No one else I'd talked to seemed to know Canada even existed. "Yes, we travelled in a ship. It took over a week to cross the ocean."

"*Vraiment?*" Solange's eyes widened.

"Yes." I told them about the swimming pool where the water all sloshed to one end, revealing the other.

"Were you frightened?" asked Solange.

"Not at all. At first it was enjoyable, very different, but in the end, it grew dull being stuck on a ship."

"So, tell me about your country," said Solange's father.

"*Papa!*" objected Solange. "We want to play."

He raised his eyebrows with the shadow of a smile. "Very well. You can tell us at dinner."

Solange grabbed my hand and dragged me off, down the hallway, past a dining room, and into her room, where she threw herself on the bed, pulling me to sit beside her.

"Where are the others?" I asked. I felt relieved that only her parents seemed to be here. Perhaps it would not be too intimidating after all.

"Oh, they will arrive soon, but we have a little time to ourselves now."

I looked around her room, which was larger than the one I shared with Frances, but still cozy. Her school paintings adorned the walls, and she'd stuck all her *Grand Images* up above her little desk. I gazed at them in awe. She had so many! Glancing her way, I saw her blushing. Solange, blushing?

"My *maman* wanted me to put them up," she said.

"It is impressive, Solange," I said. "You must be very happy."

She shrugged and looked away. "I would be happier to have a brother and sister like you," she said quietly. "Because I am the only child, my *maman et papa* are very anxious for me to succeed. It means a great deal to them, so ..." she waved the long row of *Images*.

I had no idea how to respond. I'd never heard Solange say anything to suggest she was less than perfectly content and I did not want to venture into the dangerous subject of siblings. I looked around and spied her bookcase, full of large picture books. I moved over to it and Solange joined me.

She pulled out an enormous book. "This is the prize I won last year, the *prix d'or.*"

I gazed at the book, a beautifully illustrated account of the French Revolution. "Is Marie Antoinette in it?"

"But of course." Solange flipped through the pages until we came to a full-page picture of Marie Antoinette with a towering, elaborate white wig and a gorgeous floor-length green dress.

"*Elle est si belle,*" I sighed.

We stared at the picture dreamily.

"It is a pity we do not wear garments like that anymore," I said.

Solange giggled. "I do not know about that. I would not want to wear a big white wig all the time. Think how hot that would be. And I would prefer to keep my head on my shoulders. The guillotine ... brrr."

We pored over the book, looking at pictures of Versailles and the guillotine and a furious mob tearing down the Bastille. Voices from the front of the apartment brought us back to the present.

"*Solange, vien içi.* They have arrived," called her mother.

Solange frowned. "That did not feel like very much time for us alone. But come, I must introduce you."

Regretfully, I closed the book and followed Solange back to the living room. Five people had arrived and stood with Solange's parents, all talking at once: a middle-aged couple, an old lady, a girl of about ten, and a boy a little older.

"Solange!" exclaimed the middle-aged woman. Stout, with short wavy golden hair, I assumed she must be Solange's aunt.

Solange embraced the woman, then introduced me. "*Tante Gabrielle,* this is my dear friend Margarette. And Margarette, these are my cousins Monique and Pierre, and my uncle Joseph." She hurried to a tiny woman with crimped grey hair and thick spectacles. "And this is my *grand-mère. Tout le monde, voila mon amie anglaise, Margarette.*"

The two women beckoned me closer and looked me up and down. "She is very thin," said the grandmother, reaching out to feel my arm like the witch in *Hansel and Gretel*.

"*Elle est mignonne*," said Aunt Gabrielle, favouring me with a wide smile. I'd grown used to being called cute. "*Enchantée, Margarette.*"

I smiled, feeling like an insect under a magnifying glass, and murmured that I too was enchanted.

Soon everyone settled on the couches and chairs, and Solange's mother brought out wine. The cousins perched together on a chair, eyeing me suspiciously.

I listened as they exchanged family news. Monique had recently joined her school choir; Pierre would start at the *lycée* in the fall. They chatted in a lively manner and Solange joined in from time to time. I would have preferred to return to her room and play, but she did not seem inclined to move. How different it was from my visit to Sylvie's, where we had been all alone, or indeed to the way it would have been at my house. I felt uncomfortable among these strangers and adults. Even at gatherings of my extended family, the children usually went off on their own to play.

For about an hour I sat there, engaging very little, while they prattled on. Then Solange's *maman* and her aunt bustled off to the kitchen and we all moved into the dining room. Solange indicated I should sit on the side of the table between her and her father, who naturally took the chair at the head. Her *grand-mère* sat across the table from me, on the other side of Solange's *papa*. Although the aromas from the kitchen smelled wonderful, I feared her mother would present unfamiliar and possibly unpleasant dishes I'd have trouble eating. I glanced over at Solange's place setting, to see if she'd been given a spoon, but she had a knife and fork just like me.

Her *maman* brought in a platter of odd-looking vegetables; I felt very anxious. I recognized mushrooms that I did not like and olives and grilled tomatoes and slabs of something purplish. The platter and a basket of bread circulated. As soon as Solange's *maman* sat down, everyone placed their napkins in their laps. I hurried to do the same. Conversation resumed as people helped themselves from the platter. I took bread, put it on the tablecloth beside my plate as Solange had done and then speared a couple of olives, although I suspected they would be too salty.

Her *grand-mère* watched me sternly. "No wonder you are so *maigre*, little one. You must eat more."

Solange's father put a hand on her arm. "*Maman*, she is our guest."

The old lady puffed out her cheeks, rolled her eyes dismissively, and set about eating the weird purple thing.

Perhaps to prevent any further comments about my appetite, Solange's father asked me again about Canada. Soon I found myself chattering away about how at school, girls and boys were together in class and we had both Saturday and Sunday off and how my father was a professor. My remarks provoked comments and raised eyebrows around the table, but also laughter, which reassured me. The adults all had glasses of red wine which never seemed to empty. Monique and Pierre had watered-down wine. When asked what I would like to drink, I hesitated and then said milk, as it seemed the right thing to do. Solange looked surprised but also asked for milk. I felt grateful to her; normally she would probably have had wine-and-water like her cousins. When the two glasses of milk arrived from the kitchen, I tried to ignore mine, knowing it would have the putrid chemical flavour typical of French milk. Still, better than wine.

To my relief, the main course looked entirely edible: lamb with small potatoes and green beans. As Solange's mother served the plates, she started to cut up Solange's meat. Solange murmured, *"Non, Maman."* Her mother looked like she might argue, then handed her a plate with a large slice of meat on it. I averted my eyes as she picked up her knife and fork, not wanting to embarrass her, but I couldn't help peeking to see how she managed. Her technique wasn't exactly refined, but she struggled along, tearing the meat apart with her knife and fork, and glaring at anyone who watched her. The lamb tasted wonderful and I ate heartily.

I took a sip of milk without thinking and almost gasped. It tasted good! Sweet and clean like milk at home. I quickly drained the glass, full of wonder at this small miracle, and accepted another glass to have with dessert, a fruit compote. I declined any of the white creamy sauce, suspecting it might be yoghurt.

As the meal progressed, everyone became boisterous. Solange's *papa* continued to ask questions about my life in Canada and my family, and the others seemed delighted with my responses. When they asked what I found different in Paris, I said I'd never been invited to such a fine dinner with strangers in Montreal. They all looked pleased and even her *grand-mère* commented that I had pretty manners for an English girl. I felt I'd made a good impression and Solange smiled at me proudly. To my surprise, I enjoyed myself, despite all the adults.

We were still eating dessert when my mother arrived. They invited her to join us, but she declined graciously. All the grown-ups wanted me to kiss them good-bye and Solange's *maman* insisted that I must come again soon. I left feeling on top of the world.

In the midst of telling Mom all about my visit, I burst out, "They had good milk!"

"What do you mean?"

"It tasted just like milk at home!"

"Really? Well, I must call Solange's mother and find out where they get it. That's terrific!"

No sooner did we get home than she got on the phone. I snuggled sleepily on the couch, full and happy.

She hung up the phone, turned to us with puffed out cheeks and released her breath in a whoosh. "Well, *this* you will not believe."

"What?" asked my father.

"She puts wine in the milk!"

"What?"

"I know. It's unbelievable. She said she adds a little wine to make it taste better. Can you imagine? In a child's milk?"

"But it tasted so good!" I exclaimed.

My mother rolled her eyes.

I sighed, knowing I'd never get even a drop of wine in my milk, no matter how good it might taste.

18

Cleopatra

From then on, both Sylvie and Solange came to my house fairly often, though never together, and I had repeat visits to their homes. Knowing that we would be leaving Paris at the end of June, I wanted to see as much of my friends as I could in the time remaining. Nonetheless, on a *jeudi* in early May I could not find a single friend free to play. Even my mother had plans. She'd been taking a Cordon Bleu cooking course and this was her final day.

"Bill, find something to do with Meg today. I'll be back for supper and I'll make you something special." She kissed him and rushed off, all excited.

The prospect of spending a day with my father made me cross. He always wanted to go walking. Sure, Paris was beautiful, especially in the warm weather, but I'd watched the lights reflect off the Seine and ridden up the Eiffel Tower and admired the view from the Sacré Coeur. I wanted to do something fun, like play with my friends! I crossed my arms and brooded on the unfairness of it all.

He dawdled over his breakfast. Finally, I felt his full attention settle on me. "So, we have a day to ourselves. What would you like to do?"

"I don't know." I picked at a seam on the arm of the chair. At least my mother wasn't there to scold me.

"We could go to the Tuileries. It's a beautiful day. We might see a puppet—"

"No. I'm sick of the Tuileries."

"Okay, then, how about a movie?"

I shrugged. A movie wouldn't be bad.

He flipped through the newspaper. "Aha. I'll bet you'd like this one."

"Which one?" Probably some stupid cartoon.

"Maybe not. Your mother probably wouldn't approve."

I straightened up. If my mother wouldn't approve, it might be an interesting movie, and since my mother wasn't here to disapprove … "What? What is it?"

He shook his head. "Oh, I don't know."

"What movie? Daaad?"

"*Cleopatra.*"

I gasped. Cleopatra, queen of ancient Egypt. I knew about Egypt from Frances, who'd read *Mara, Daughter of the Nile* a dozen times. My mother had declared the book inappropriate for me; I could hardly wait to read it.

"I don't know," my dad continued. "It might be too grown-up for you. But Elizabeth Taylor and Richard Burton are in it."

"Elizabeth Taylor!" That did it. My mother had told me a million times that Elizabeth Taylor was the most beautiful woman in the world. How could I possibly miss a chance to see her in the role of Cleopatra! "Dad, we must go. There's nothing I'd rather do than see *Cleopatra*. Please, please, please?"

"I've heard it's quite long," He scratched his head, but the twinkle in his eye gave him away. "All right." He grinned at me.

We ate an early lunch and set off. As the cinema was quite far away, we took the Metro. I always felt nervous descending the long staircases into the underground. A layer of grime covered the walls and platforms, the air roiled with the hot smells of the trains, and the more unpleasant odours of urine and French tobacco. The train roared into the station and we clambered on, then switched trains at a huge station, walking for ages along echoing corridors.

But as soon as the movie began, I was transported to a world of intrigue and love and Elizabeth Taylor, sublime as the calculating and heart-stoppingly gorgeous Cleopatra. I paid little attention to any of the men in the film, having eyes only for the queen. Elizabeth Taylor wore a different costume in every scene, and it didn't bother me a bit that some looked like the outfits worn by models on magazine covers, although I preferred the swirling see-through gowns and golden headdresses.

Cleopatra's entrance into Rome, preceded by a wild parade of acrobats and dancers, coloured smoke, and exotic music, was brilliant. It went on for even longer than the Santa Claus parade in Montreal! Best of all, the procession held the Romans, who had not taken Cleopatra seriously, spellbound. Then she arrived high on a float as large as a building, clad all in gold, sitting before a towering sphinx, the greatest queen who'd ever lived.

I loved her mischievous ways. She first appeared in the movie rolled up in a rug and later drifted towards Mark Antony on a barge, surrounded by beautiful young women and rippling silken sails. Oh, to be Cleopatra, so irresistible and exquisite, to wear such stunning garments, to have Roman emperors so madly in love that they behaved foolishly in battle. And to have so much gold: golden thrones and beds and pools and sceptres and gowns and eyelids. Ahhh ...

At the end, tears streamed from my eyes as she coolly placed her hand in the basket of figs and only winced when the deadly asp bit her: so proud and free and oh so beautiful, even on her tomb. I barely heard my father's gentle snores. When the lights came up, I didn't want to leave, I wanted to stay and watch all four hours again and again and again.

"Look at the time!" Dad said, jerking to his feet. "We'd better hurry or we'll be late for dinner."

I followed him along the street, lost in Egyptian dreams.

A great crowd streamed down the steps down to the Metro. I saw them as soldiers carrying me on a wave of adoration. My father clung to my hand.

"Damn," Dad muttered. "It's rush hour."

People certainly did seem to be in a rush. The platform was packed, and we sidled along the wall. A train roared in and the crowd surged towards the doors only to be shoved back by people pouring out of the train.

My father looked a bit pale. "We'll wait for the next train," he said.

The platform cleared a little. Spotting a candy machine, I persuaded my father to give me a franc so I could buy a round tin of hard candies. I loved the sharp orange flavour and the pretty pictures on the containers. As I leaned down to pick up the tin, another train rushed in. The crowd heaved me along the platform. Glancing about I could see only legs, shopping bags and parcels. No sign of my father.

"Meg!" I heard him shout.

I fought against the flow in the direction of his voice, panicking now as the force of the crowd pushed me towards the train. I could hardly breathe. I caught a glimpse of my father hanging on to the door of the train as the crowd jostled, trying to push him inside.

"Dad!" I shouted, certain the doors would close and either crush him or carry him off, leaving me alone in the middle of the mob.

"Meg," he hollered.

Hands seized me, wrenching me off my feet into the air. *"Attention,"* a woman shouted. "The girl must go with her father. *Regardez la!"*

My father caught sight of me. "Meg! Over here. *Aidez-moi,"* he implored the crowd.

Hands grabbed me, carrying me through the press and launching me into the snarl of bodies inside the train. My father released the door and it shuddered closed. He held out his hand, I reached between two men and our fingers touched as the train rumbled out of the station.

Three stops later he'd managed to squeeze his way through the crowd to my side; he clutched me to him. "Are you all right?" he whispered, his face damp with sweat.

I nodded, my legs quivering as I leaned against him.

He did not release my hand until we'd made our way through the steamy tunnels at the transfer station onto another packed train and, finally, out onto the platform at *Château-Rouge*, our neighbourhood station.

"My God," he said. "That was awful. I was—"

I squeezed his hand. "It's okay, Dad." I knew he'd been scared; I also knew he wouldn't want to admit it.

We walked the rest of the way in silence. By the time we reached *rue Nicolet*, the Metro nightmare had faded, and I was floating along the Nile again.

"Where have you been?" asked my mother as we reached the Room With A View. The kitchen looked like a disaster zone, with pots and pans and bowls all over the place. My mother stood at the stove, stirring something that smelled absolutely delicious. She glanced over at us and her eyes widened, but she didn't stop stirring. "Bill? Are you all right?"

"God," he said. "We got caught in rush hour on the Metro. I almost lost Meg."

My mother blanched. "Where were you?"

This was the moment of truth. My mother would not be pleased that I'd seen a scantily clad Elizabeth Taylor luring Roman emperors into her bed. I knew that, but Dad and I had not talked about what we would say.

He poured some whiskey into a glass. "We went to see *Cleopatra*."

My mother's eyebrows rushed together. "And how was it?" she asked tightly.

"Long," he said.

Long? "It was magnificent," I breathed. "Oh Mom, you wouldn't believe. Elizabeth Taylor *is* the most beautiful woman in the world. You're right. And you should have seen the costumes and the barge. She rode into Rome on a gigantic sphinx and Antony just fell in love with her and then she put her hand in a basket of figs and let an asp poison her. It was the most wonderful movie I've ever seen."

"Hmmm," she said, focusing her full attention on stirring. "Hmm. Well." Her voice softened. "I'm glad you enjoyed it."

Over the top of his glass, my father winked at me. "What's for supper? It smells divine."

"You just wait and see," said my mother.

I couldn't stop talking about *Cleopatra*. At first my mother seemed amused, but soon lost interest. She was putting on a show of her own at dinner.

"Enough about Elizabeth Taylor," she snapped as she served us asparagus soup. She waited as we tasted it. "What do you think?"

My father closed his eyes. "Margaret, it's sublime."

I forced myself to swallow a mouthful. Asparagus held no appeal for me, but I had to admit it wasn't bad.

"It's delicious, Mom," said Frances.

"Uh huh," said Neil, spooning it in so fast I thought he might choke.

Mom smiled and sipped her soup delicately. "It is rather nice isn't it? It took two days to prepare. I made the stock at the school and finished the soup here."

"Amazing," breathed my father. "Children, your mother is the best cook in the world!"

She blushed. "Hardly. But I'll tell you something, it's a lot easier to be a great chef when you have a troop of staff cleaning up after you. Look at this kitchen!"

Frances and Neil glanced miserably at the counters, piled high with pots and pans. They shared the job of washing dishes. I set the table.

"At the school every time the chef finishes with a pot, someone whips it away to wash. The place is absolutely full of cookware, pots and pans of every shape and size, all gleaming. It's fantastic."

It sounded sort of stupid to me. All that fuss about cooking. I glanced over at the stove, hoping maybe she'd made artichokes. Instead she ladled out bowls of *coq au vin*, which was just a fancy chicken stew, too rich and full of red wine for me. I munched on bread and toyed with the odd chunk of chicken. Everyone else went into raptures.

"You should have seen Cleopatra's palace," I said. "She had a great indoor pool, kind of like a hot bath and she received messengers from Rome floating there."

My father gave my foot a nudge under the table. Cleopatra had been naked in the bath, although submerged.

My mother said, "Yes, well, it sounds like quite the movie. Can I please have some more wine, Bill?"

"What was Antony like?" asked Frances.

"He was okay. Wore a very short tunic which looked a bit silly."

"That was Richard Burton, right Dad?" asked Frances.

"Hmmm? Yeah. Meg's right, he did look a bit silly showing his bare legs like a schoolboy."

My mother rose. "Now we'll have a very light fennel and radish salad."

I frowned. My mother made a great salad, usually, but I didn't care for radishes. "What's fennel?"

"It's a kind of bulb, a bit like an onion, but licorice-flavoured."

I loved licorice, but in a salad? "They ate a lot of grapes in the movie and drank out of jewelled gold cups." Drifting back to Egypt, I took a sip of my chemical milk and grimaced.

"The meat is so tender," said Frances.

Neil nodded appreciatively. "And the gravy—"

"It's a sauce," said my mother as she presented the salad.

I could tell she didn't feel she was getting quite the attention she deserved. "So Mom," I asked, "you're a Cordon Bleu chef now?"

She laughed. "Well, I've finished the course and I've learned a lot." She raised her glass. "And I want to thank you all for putting up with my experiments and my absences. I've had a lot of fun!"

"To Mom, the best chef in the world!" said my brother. He was drinking wine. How did that happen?

We all toasted and cheered and ate the salad, which wasn't too bad. Then the dessert appeared—a crème caramel—all soggy and jiggly.

"I'm tired," I said.

My mother still got a worried look when I said things like that, even though everyone agreed I was MUCH BETTER.

"It's late. Off you go to bed, then." She kissed me, smelling of wine.

In the dark bedroom, I heard the slap of waves against my barge and imagined silken maidens bringing me grapes.

19

Playing the Queen

The next day I rushed over to Solange and Danielle in the school courtyard. The renovations had been completed on our old school, so we no longer had the long walk at the start and end of day.

"I did something very special yesterday," I told them.

Solange's eyes widened. "What?"

"My father took me to see the film *Cleopatra*."

Neither of them looked particularly impressed.

"It was the most marvellous experience I have ever had," I breathed.

"Tell us," said Solange.

"Well, for one thing it was really an adult film. My mother would not have approved."

"Ooh la la," they said together.

"It is the story of Cleopatra, the beautiful queen of ancient Egypt, starring Elizabeth Taylor," I began. They listened, rapt, as I recounted the events in the movie. It took me the whole day to tell the story. I paused when Madame called us in for class, resumed at morning, lunch, and afternoon recesses, and barely finished by the time we were dismissed. I had a reputation as a pretty good storyteller and as the word spread of "Margarette's spectacular experience," other girls gathered around. I lingered on descriptions of the settings and especially Cleopatra's costumes. Her gold-leafed gown brought very satisfying gasps from my audience.

"*Quelle histoire!*" murmured Solange. "How I wish I could see this film, but my *maman* would never allow it. Did you see the asps? What did they look like?"

"Very small, like large black worms, but filled with deadly poison."

"Ahhh." She shivered. "We should play the story, don't you think?"

"Yes! Of course. We must do that, Solange. A brilliant idea." Why hadn't I thought of this? It would be the most elaborate and stunning game of Pretend ever. I walked home thinking about it and was so excited that I stayed out on the street and got Patrick and Josée to play with me. I'd forsaken them almost entirely now that I had new friends, but they seemed excited and willing to take the parts of a soldier and a serving maid. I, of course, played Cleopatra.

The next day, the schoolyard became my grand stage. Most of the girls in my class gathered to watch us act out scenes that only I had seen. For a second, Solange looked irritated when I claimed the lead role, but her brow cleared as I explained that I looked just like Cleopatra with my dark hair and straight bangs. I did not mention that I lacked Elizabeth Taylor's bosom and soft curves. No one else had seen the movie, so they had to take my word that I was almost her spitting image.

"All Egyptians have dark hair and dark eyes, and Cleopatra's is cut just like mine," I told Solange. "But some of the Romans are fair. Solange, you must be Mark Antony, for Cleopatra loves him above all else." I smiled encouragingly. "And he was a great warrior." I thought it best not to mention the silly tunic and bare legs.

"Very well," said Solange. "I shall lead armies into battle."

"But first, Julius Caesar falls in love with her! Danielle, you must be Caesar. He is a very great emperor, though older than Mark Antony."

Since Solange had agreed to play a male role, Danielle graciously took on Caesar.

"We will begin with the first meeting," I declared. "Cleopatra is carried in, rolled up in a rug. Caesar is astonished."

"But there is no rug," said Danielle.

"We must pretend!"

Other girls eagerly volunteered to be the servants who carried the rug. "You must pick me up, pretending I am inside the rug and then unroll me before Caesar."

This proved an awkward undertaking, but eventually the servants managed to lift me. I tried to stay stiff as a board. Then they dumped me on the ground. I rolled to Caesar's feet, trying to look both commanding and seductive.

Solange burst out laughing.

I felt miffed, but when the other girls collapsed in giggles, I couldn't help laughing myself.

I sat up. "It was funny in the movie too! Imagine, a queen in a rug." We giggled all the way back to class.

Cleopatra obsessed me. At every break, I rushed out, ready to embark on another scene. The arrival of Cleopatra in Rome called for a parade in which the whole class could participate. Although I disapproved of some of their antics, I tried to concentrate on looking regal and gliding across the cobblestones as though I were on a sphinx float.

"The crowd is absolutely amazed by her entrance," I coached.

The few girls playing the Roman crowd gasped and opened their eyes as wide as they could.

"And Caesar is delighted," I told Danielle.

She grinned and nodded. Sometimes it was hard to imagine that this little French girl with brown hair and a turned-up nose could be Caesar, but I persisted.

My favourite scene was Cleopatra's death. Sylvie played my attendant and brought the asp-ridden basket of figs— her lunchbox. I sat on the ground leaning against a tree and extended my hand. Sylvie started to sniffle.

"Sylvie," I hissed. "It is just a game. I am not really going to die."

She nodded, gazing at me with sorrowful adoration.

I gasped and shuddered as the pretend asp bit me.

Sylvie cried out, "*Non, non, ma reine!*" Perfect.

Our heartfelt performances were interrupted by Madame calling us in to class. I found it difficult to concentrate on the wretched embroidery. Solange had finished hers and it looked pretty. I had to complete mine. Soon our year of schooling would end, and we would receive our final rankings. I longed to be among the top girls and now it seemed I might just make it. I had received several *Grande Images,* turned in perfect *dictées,* and now brought a sense of drama to the *resumés* we declaimed in class. Since I'd had excellent marks in arithmetic and gym for most of the year, I thought

I had a pretty good chance of receiving some form of honour. Of course, Solange would take the *prix d'or*. Indeed, I hoped she would, given how much her parents wanted her to succeed.

In class I tried to focus on schoolwork, but I lived for the next instalment of *Cleopatra*. After a few days of playing out the story in bits and pieces, I grew frustrated by the fact that we had to pretend absolutely everything.

"It would be so much more effective if we had crowns and baskets of figs and sceptres," I moaned to Solange.

She laughed. "Yes, you are right, but that would be impossible."

"Would it? What if we made costumes and props and actually performed it as a play?"

Solange looked dubious. "How could we do that?"

My imagination ran wild. "We could make crowns from cardboard and paint them gold and... oh, think of it Solange, if we had golden gowns and armour and swords. It would be *un vrai spectacle*."

Solange nodded. "That would be *magnifique, Margarette, mais très difficile, n'est ce pas?*"

"Let me think upon it," I said, a little irritated at her practicality.

I spoke to my mother in wheedling tones. "Mom, you know how we're all playing at *Cleopatra* at school?"

"Uh huh."

"I was thinking, wouldn't it be amazing if we actually put on a play, with costumes and props and everything, like in a real theatre?"

"Uh huh." She pecked away at the typewriter keys.

"So, I wondered whether maybe you could help me make the props and find costumes and we could perform it here." I waited expectantly for her response.

She stopped typing and looked at me. "Sorry?"

I repeated myself in enthusiastic tones.

"That sounds very complicated," she said. "Where would we get props and costumes?"

"We could buy some gold paint and use cardboard and I could get everyone to borrow dress-up clothes—"

"Everyone? How many girls are you talking about? Where would you perform? This isn't exactly a theatre."

She had a point. I tried to imagine dragging a sphinx into the Room With A View. We could manage without the sphinx. "Well I don't know for sure how many, but—"

"We can talk about it later." She frowned. "I have to finish this article."

That evening when I raised the subject again, she said, "I'll buy you the gold paint and you can borrow some clothes, but you'll have to make the crowns and things yourself. And you'll have to find somewhere else to perform. There just isn't enough space here."

"But where?" I moaned.

"What about at school? In the courtyard?"

That sounded unlikely to me, but I decided to discuss it with Solange. Meanwhile we could start preparing for our *vrai spectacle*.

The next day I skipped into the school courtyard and announced my plans. The girls listened, then erupted in shrieks of excitement. The idea of wearing costumes and golden crowns and actually recreating the majesty and spectacle of the film gripped them almost as much as it did me. We spent most of the day discussing details.

"My mother has a gold dress with beads," said Sylvie. "I will ask if I can borrow it."

"*Merveilleux!*" I exclaimed. I could already see myself in a beautiful golden gown studded with pearls.

Someone offered a covered basket for the asps, normally used to store sewing materials. Another girl said she could paint our eyelids; her mother had a great store of make-up. The rug would prove more challenging. We had one at *6 rue Nicolet* that I thought would serve, but I knew my mother would never allow us to use anything from the house. The landlady Madame Dufrèche would not approve.

At the end of the day I snatched a moment to talk to Solange.

"There is one problem," I said. "Where can we perform our *spectacle*?"

"Perhaps at your house?"

I shook my head. "There is not enough room."

She frowned. "This is a challenge."

I waited, hoping she would have an inspiration.

She shrugged. "Perhaps it is impossible."

"No, it cannot be impossible!" I made a great show of concentrating, then said, "Do you think Madame might let us perform it here? As an end of school *spectacle*, like the *pièce de Noël*?" I tried not to sound too hopeful.

She shook her head dismissively. "No, absolutely not."

"Why not?" I felt like crying.

"There is no precedent. It is not the tradition of the school to perform plays at the end of the year. No, it is impossible." She shrugged again, as though she didn't really care.

"But, Solange, you know how everyone longs to do this. The whole class. It would be so *incroyable*. Could you not ask Madame? If anyone could persuade her, it would be you. She adores you."

Solange rolled her eyes. Perhaps I had gone a little too far. Madame did not *adore* anyone.

At that moment, Solange's *maman* appeared.

"*Bonjour, Margarette. Comment ça va?*" She smiled at me.

"*Très bien, et vous?*" I responded listlessly.

"*Très bien.* Come, Solange, we must hurry." She took Solange's hand.

As they turned to go, Solange winked at me. "Do not look so sad, Margarette. We will find a way. Let me think on it."

That afternoon I dragged my mother to the *Prixunic* to buy paint and cardboard. The haughty shop attendants assured us that the *Prixunic* did not stock such items, implying that gold paint—I mean GOLD paint—was somehow beneath the lofty standards of their store. My mother pursed her lips and we set off down the street to the *quincaillerie* (hardware store) where, after much negotiating, we obtained a small can of gold paint. My mother grumbled about the cost all the way home and I stayed very quiet.

The following day, I waited anxiously to see if Solange had any ideas.

"It is no use," she said. "I cannot ask Madame such a thing. She would think I was an *imbecile. Je suis désolée, Margarette.*" She did not sound desolated at all.

I felt miserable.

But by recess, I had recovered. Somehow, we would find a performance space. Meanwhile, there was the whole *mise en scène* to be figured out. I once more began issuing directions and organizing the girls into battalions. I almost forgot we had no place to perform, as I rehearsed scenes by day and crafted golden bracelets and diadems by night. Sometimes I got so wound up with excitement I couldn't sleep and thrashed around until my dear sister ordered me to "Shut up and stay still!"

A week later, when I called everyone to rehearse at recess, Solange said, "Can we not do something else for a change? I am weary of *Cleopatra*."

I felt as though she'd slapped my face. "Weary? Solange, we are preparing our *grand spectacle*."

"Your *grand spectacle*, you mean." She faced me, hands on her hips, her face set. "We have done nothing but play *Cleopatra* for weeks. I would just like to do something else for a change."

"If we want to present a fine performance we must rehearse." I glared at her.

"I do not care about the performance," she said. "I am tired of it."

"What do you mean? If you do not rehearse, you cannot be in the play!"

She shrugged and walked away.

Swallowing a great lump in my throat, I turned to Sylvie. "Let us do the scene in which you bring the message about Antony," I said, determined not to show how hurt I felt. Sylvie smiled and threw herself down before me, as slaves did in ancient Egypt.

My eyes followed Solange as she crossed the courtyard whispering with another girl. I did not speak to her for the rest of the day. She knew how important this play was to me. How could she dismiss it?

The next day, Solange smiled at me when I arrived at school. I ignored her. If she did not want to be part of my *grand spectacle,* so be it. She was probably just jealous because I had the role of Cleopatra and for once was calling the shots. Well, I could do the play without her. I had plenty of friends now. I did not need Solange.

20

Fête D'Adieu

At school, I pretended not to care about Solange's desertion and continued with rehearsals. At home, I moped. Solange did not care about me. I could never be her friend again after her despicable behaviour. How could she ruin my *grand spectacle*? Now not only did I lack a place to perform, I also lacked a Mark Antony. No doubt Solange was very pleased with herself for having single-handedly destroyed all my handiwork. I could not let her undermine my plans. The thought of her gloating in triumph made me grit my teeth.

"What's the matter, honey?" Mom asked after school one day.

"Nothing."

"Oh, come on, something's wrong. You're awfully quiet." She ruffled my hair.

I stared at the apple in front of me. I'd taken one bite.

"Is it to do with your play?"

Clearly, she was not going to leave me to sulk. I did not want to tell her of Solange's betrayal. Still, she sounded awfully sympathetic. Maybe I could turn this to my advantage. "Well, yes," I sighed. "It's coming along well, but we have no place to perform." I looked up at her mournfully.

"Hmmm. Did you ask Madame about doing it at school?"

I shook my head. "No, Solange said she would never allow it."

"Knowing Madame, Solange is probably right. What other ideas have you had?"

"None. The only place I can imagine we could perform would be here. You're the only parents who'd let us."

She sighed. "It's really important to you, isn't it?"

To my surprise, tears filled my eyes. It *was* important, in more ways than I wanted my mother to know. "Yes," I mumbled.

"Well, maybe you could do it here ..."

Despite her tentative tone, my spirits soared. "Really? Really, Mom?"

She frowned. "I don't know. We don't really have enough space, but—"

Inspiration struck me. "Hey, it could be my good-bye party! I mean we're leaving at the end of June. I could have a final party, couldn't I? And we'd perform our play!"

She bit at her lip. "Well, I suppose you could have a party, but you can't invite the entire Roman Empire or the Egyptian Court or whatever you call it."

"Ten girls. I could do it with ten."

"TEN? That's way too many." Her voice rose. "Besides, you know perfectly well a lot of the mothers won't allow them and I don't want to spend the whole of next week on the phone persuading hoity-toity Parisian women to let their daughters come to your party."

"Okay, okay. Not ten. Let me think. Eight?"

"Five."

I ran through the roles. Five, plus me would be six. "I could probably do it with five. But can we really do it here? And have a party? Please?"

She sighed. "Oh, all right. Five girls and a performance of *Cleopatra*." She shook her head as if to say *I must be out of my mind*, but I saw the hint of a smile on her lips.

I cheered right up. There'd been tension in the schoolyard; the girls clearly felt torn between Solange and me. Solange had more clout than I did. She'd been around longer, had more friends and better marks—and I, after all, was about to leave forever. Danielle, to her credit, had stuck with *Cleopatra*, but she watched longingly as Solange sauntered off to do entirely inconsequential things at recess. Several of the other girls had lost interest in the performance and resumed following in Solange's wake. But now that we had a place to perform, the whole undertaking would take on new life! The girls would be thrilled at the thought of being invited to a *fête chez moi*.

Still, I could only include five girls. And I had to replace Mark Antony. I tossed and turned again that night, until Frances whacked me with a pillow.

In the morning I dawdled on my way to school. The din of cars honking, brakes screeching and men shouting barely registered as I made my way past the *pâtisserie* and down the wide boulevard. As I sidestepped a rather unpleasant pile of dog poo, I reached a decision. I would not tell the whole class about the party. So many of them would feel left out. We could continue rehearsing the big scenes just for fun. I would replace Solange with Marie-Claire, who loved to act and was tall. She had nothing like Solange's wit and quickness, but one had to make sacrifices for art. Vincent van Gogh had sacrificed his ear! I would sacrifice an almost perfect Mark Antony (except for her gender and her tendency to make me giggle). The show must go on.

My steps slowed as I neared the huge door marked *Filles*. I felt pretty confident that Danielle would continue as Caesar, especially if I told her about the party, and Sylvie would never desert me, so I had the three lead roles and Iris, my maidservant. With a couple of others to play the crowds, armies, messengers, Octavius, Octavia (the wretched woman who had the nerve to marry Mark Antony while he was in Rome), other Roman generals, and slaves, we'd manage.

I arrived too late to rehearse before school and spent the morning silently appraising the girls in the class, trying to choose two other girls to complete the real cast. No one could play so many roles with any success. My eyes lingered on Solange. She could do it; she could do anything, but she was *weary* of *Cleopatra*. When she glanced up with a tentative smile, I turned away, angry to be caught showing the slightest interest. In the end, I chose Nicole, who was hefty and quite strong, and Valérie, a pretty girl with dark curly hair. They were far from brilliant, but they would have to do.

By now it was June; only a few weeks of school remained. My mother and I decided the party would take place a week before the end of school. The gold props stood ready. I'd painted jewels on the crown and bracelets and felt quite pleased with the result. A gold stick with a ball jammed on the end would serve as a sceptre. Cleopatra would arrive wrapped in a blanket. Sylvie's mother's dress proved a disappointment. It was short and fitted but hung like a sack on me. Rallying, I decided to wear one of my mother's nightgowns with a big beaded belt. I told Sylvie she should wear the gold dress, even if it would make her look more like a cabaret performer than an Egyptian maidservant.

Once more I created invitations, with no help from Marie-Laurence this time. When I delivered them to my five friends, word spread instantly through the schoolyard. Girls who had faithfully rehearsed with us came to me in tears, begging to be included. I felt horrible as I explained, "We do not have room for the whole cast. *Je suis desolée.*" I truly did feel desolated.

When Solange heard, her face turned pale and her lip quivered. As I hurried out of the schoolyard after school, she caught my arm. "Margarette," she whispered. "I am sorry for being so mean. I would like to be in your *grand spectacle.* May I?"

"I am afraid not. You have missed too many rehearsals," I said coldly.

"But I did not realize you would really perform the play."

I shrugged and strode away. I knew she just wanted to come to my party. Well, she should have thought of that before.

When I gave my mother the list of phone numbers so she could call the girls' mothers, she frowned. "What about Solange?"

"We are no longer friends," I fiddled with a corner of my crown that kept folding over.

"Since when?" She stared at me.

"Since she decided she was too grand to perform in my play."

"Oh. That's too bad. You were so close."

"These things happen." I hurried downstairs to my room, afraid I might start crying. I did not want to think about the friendship I'd lost or Solange's wounded look when I refused to let her back into the cast. It was her fault. She'd betrayed me. She deserved to suffer.

The next day Nicole came to me in tears. Her mother would not allow her to come to the party. "She is horrible. She says I cannot visit the house of an English family," she sobbed.

Once again girls surrounded me, begging to be invited in Nicole's place. Solange watched from a distance, her face sad. I began to wish I'd never come up with this idea, but I could not let my dream of *Cleopatra* die! When Émilie pestered me all day, I gave in and asked her to play all the Roman messengers and slaves.

After school, I asked my mother to call Émilie's *maman*.

She sat me down at the table and said, "Meg, why don't you ask Solange instead? Her mother called me this afternoon. Solange is very upset that you are no longer friends—"

"That's not true. She just can't stand the idea that she won't be at my party." I glowered at her.

"How do you know?" She gazed at me with sad eyes; I felt I had disappointed her.

"Because. She refused to rehearse. She wanted nothing to do with *Cleopatra*. She was Mark Antony, you know, and she just up and left. I had to replace her, and no one could play the part like Solange." My voice trembled.

"Meg, not everyone loves acting as much as you do. Not everyone is as good at it or as imaginative—"

"Solange is! But she just didn't want to be in the play. She knew how much it meant to me, but she just didn't care."

She stroked my hand. "She does now. She's very sorry about what she did. In a couple of weeks, you'll never see her again. Can't you forgive her?"

I wrenched my arm away and jumped up. "NO. I can't. Maybe I'm mean but so was she. I won't let her be in the play. I won't!" I rushed down the stairs.

This time I did dissolve in tears when I got to my room. I hated everyone. Why was Mom making it sound like it was all my fault? Like I was being cruel? It wasn't fair.

Mom called Émilie's mother and she agreed to let her daughter attend my *fête d'adieu*. I'd always been intrigued by the fact that the French had two words for good-bye, one that meant *I'll see you again* and the other which meant *good-bye forever*. I felt a lump in my throat at the thought of never again seeing Sylvie and Danielle and the kind lady at the *boulangerie* and Madame Wax and Marie-Laurence and Patrick and Josée and the Haywards and Sylvie's *maman et papa* and François. Still, my *fête d'adieu* would be spectacular! And I would not miss Solange at all.

I barely slept the night before the party, worried as I was about the performance. In the morning I dragged myself to the *boulangerie* to get our baguettes, nodding without expression as the *madame* handed over the loaves. Even the heady smell of fresh bread did not arouse any appetite.

When I rose from the breakfast table after only a few bites, Mom said, "Are you all right?" She gazed at me, her brow furrowed.

"I'm fine," I muttered. "I'm not sick!"

She raised her eyebrows.

Frances had offered to help me get dressed and do my make-up. She snapped at me when my eyelids fluttered as she applied heavy blue eye shadow. "Keep still!"

When she'd finished, I gazed in the mirror. I looked more like a doll than Elizabeth Taylor.

My mother's nightgown hung on me.

"Do you want to stuff one of my bras and wear it?" Frances asked, her tone bright and helpful.

That just sounded gross, but maybe it would make me appear more seductive? We tried it.

"Yes, that makes you look more grown up," she said.

The bra felt uncomfortable, but I was prepared to suffer for the cause, and it did add curves where I had none whatsoever.

The whole family helped clear the Room With A View, pushing the table into the corner and setting up chairs on one side of the room. We would use the staircase as an entranceway. I gazed critically at the empty space, thinking "stage" to myself. It didn't look like a stage but the Louis XV armchair with its gold velvet upholstery made a reasonable throne.

As two o'clock approached, I felt a rush of excitement. The props were laid out in my bedroom: two spears (handles from our broom and mop, with gold cardboard blades taped to the tops), a dagger (kitchen knife), the sewing basket for the asp scene, gold helmets for Mark Antony and Caesar (that had a distinct similarity to baseball caps), the blanket-cum-rug and a tray of pewter wine glasses for the servant to carry around. I nodded approvingly and scurried downstairs to await the arrival of my players and their parents.

Danielle arrived looking like Charlie Chaplin in a suit of her father's. I swallowed as I greeted her. Not much similarity to Caesar, but never mind. Sylvie bulged in all the wrong places in her mother's cocktail dress. Marie-Claire, to whom I had confided details of Richard Burton's costume in an ill-considered moment, wore shorts that disappeared beneath a man's white shirt. Valérie and Émilie both arrived in party dresses.

"But where are your costumes?" I asked. "You were to wear simple clothes in dark colours!" I tried to suppress my rage.

"My *maman* insisted I dress for a party. It is my best dress," whispered Valérie so that her mother could not hear.

Émilie stared at me blankly. "Oh. I forgot."

Idiots! I wanted to punch them.

My mother gave me a warning look. "Meg, let's get everyone upstairs so you can begin." She led the parents up, chatting politely.

"Look," I heard Marie-Claire whisper, "Margarette has made herself a bosom!"

The girls collapsed in giggles. I felt my face flush.

"Let us begin!" I commanded. I took them to my room, showed them the props and explained that they had to listen very carefully on the staircase for their entrance cues and enter with style.

Valérie said, "What is an entrance cue?"

My excitement had drained away, replaced by something like terror. I had an impulse to tear off my nightgown—and the increasingly uncomfortable bra—and run out into the street.

My mother appeared in the doorway. "Are you ready to begin?" she whispered. Her eyes travelled over the cast and she made a little noise, a sort of snuffle-cough that could well have been a smothered giggle. She clamped her lips together.

I took a deep breath and donned my crown. This was it, the moment I'd been working toward for the past six weeks. I would be the noble, gorgeous, powerful Cleopatra. If the rest of the cast did not quite come up to the standard I set, so be it. The audience could use their imaginations.

"Danielle, go up and sit on the throne! Valérie and Émilie, we will walk as far up the stairs as we can without being seen. You can carry me the last few steps."

Danielle obediently tripped up the stairs. I heard a smattering of applause. Valérie and Émilie gazed at me nervously.

"I don't think I can do it," said Émilie.

Why had I agreed to let her join the cast? "Yes, you can," I growled menacingly. "You don't have to say anything. Now, follow me." I grabbed the blanket and tried to wrap myself in it head to toe, then realized I wouldn't be able to walk up the stairs wound up in a blanket. I disentangled myself and climbed the stairs until we were almost in view, then made another attempt. The stairs made it awkward. Silence reigned above.

"Am I all covered?" I whispered through the wool.

"Cover her hair," murmured Valérie.

"Be careful!" I whispered. I did not want the crown disturbed.

They fumbled with the blanket. "There. Perfect," said Émilie, much too loudly.

The audience laughed. I felt suffocated. "Now lift me."

We had not practiced on stairs. The girls grunted as I tried to remain ramrod stiff. For a second I thought they might drop me; I imagined crashing down the stairs and breaking bones. Is that what they meant when they said, "break a leg"?

They bumped me up the stairs and dropped me on the floor but forgot to unroll me. I lay there swathed in blanket, waiting, but nothing happened. I tried to roll across the floor in what I hoped was the general direction of the throne, but the blanket did not come loose. I bumped into something. Then I thrashed about in a sweat until I'd freed my feet and hands. I struggled to disentangle myself from the blanket. My crown, crushed beyond recognition, fell on the floor. Danielle rose and knelt, looking into my eyes. I could see her struggling to hold back giggles as she said "Cleopatra! Queen of the Nile. I am astonished."

As I tried to rise nymph-like from the floor, I felt something snap. Glancing down I saw my sister's bra flatten and the stuffing fall out at my feet. My eyes felt gluey. The eye shadow seemed to have gotten into them; a blue blur obscured everything. I held out a hand to Caesar. Danielle kissed it, looking like a clown. I wanted to die.

The performance went from bad to worse. The blades on the spears flopped over, Sylvie dropped the tray of pewter goblets. Marie-Claire forgot all her lines. The bra bounced against me as I tried to glide on my non-existent sphinx into Rome. On more than one occasion the audience burst out laughing, though my sister tried valiantly to shush them.

Finally, we got to the scene with the asps. I had real tears in my eyes as the asp bit me, not because I was sad at the thought of dying but because I was so deeply disappointed with the way the performance had gone. Still, Sylvie rose magnificently to the occasion, declaiming *"La reine est morte"* with a tremble in her voice. The audience applauded wildly—out of all proportion to the quality of the *spectacle* they had witnessed—and we bowed and grinned.

The girls enjoyed the party, stuffing themselves with pastries and Fanta. Their mothers said kind things about the performance, which I did not believe. Sylvie smiled cheerfully at me. She did not understand what a disaster my *grand spectacle* had been. As I munched on a tasteless tart, I thought of Solange with an aching feeling. I missed her terribly. Why had I been so mean to her? For what? A stupid performance, which had nothing of the magic I so badly wanted to capture. By the time everyone left, I could barely murmur, *"au revoir."*

21

Les Prix

My family heaped praise on both the production of *Cleopatra* and my performance as Queen of the Nile.

"I loved the way you floated across the room on your arrival in Rome," said Frances, her eyes shining.

"It was terrific, Meg. Better than the film!" My father beamed at me. I rolled my eyes. As if I didn't know better.

"Your death was quite lovely," said my mother. "You exercised great restraint."

"Bravo!" shouted Neil, as though I were a flamenco dancer.

They chattered about the creative props and the organization the entire spectacle had required.

"It was pretty funny when you couldn't get out of the blanket." Neil chuckled.

"Neil!" My mother and Frances admonished him.

A few days earlier, I'd have taken offense at this remark. Now I no longer cared. The moment the guests departed, I lost all interest in *Cleopatra*, or at least in my enactment of the story. It had been a fiasco, an unintentional tragicomedy, and I simply felt relieved to have it over with. Just as well. I'd barely been able to get the show on before the entire household became swept up in the whirlwind of preparations for departure.

In a week, we would leave *6 rue Nicolet*. My sister would go to Normandy to live with a French family for the summer. Neil had a placement on a youth project in Norway. My parents and I would summer in the south of France on the Atlantic coast, sharing a villa with family friends who had three daughters. I was close friends with the middle girl, Nancy, and looked forward to seeing her again. But it seemed far away, unreal. I did not really want to leave Paris.

Guilt over my behaviour towards Solange weighed heavy on me. My rage at her betrayal had evaporated; I tried to re-ignite it, to recall my anger and hurt, but I could not. Her crime seemed tiny compared to mine. She had grown weary of *Cleopatra*. Well, so had I now. She had only wanted to do something else. Whereas I had spurned her. I had refused to invite her to my *fête*. She must have been so hurt. I had been cruel—to my best friend. And now it was too late to make amends. We would leave Paris and the ache in my heart would be with me forever.

I sank into gloom as my mother bustled about packing trunks to be shipped home. No one noticed. I'd had my moment of glory (or disgrace); now the family turned their attention elsewhere. Frances and Neil had completed their classes and were studying for exams, Frances furiously, Neil in a less intense fashion. My father disappeared into the streets of Paris to revisit his favourite haunts by day and worked late into the night finishing his book. I crept about a house in chaos.

At school, tension filled the classroom. I finished my embroidery, working alongside Sylvie now. Solange had restored Danielle to her position as prime companion. The classroom was the scene of intense competition. No one spoke or giggled or made faces behind Madame's back anymore. Unlike in Canada, where no serious work occurred during the last week of school, in Paris we had innumerable tests and *dictées* as the final day approached, the Day of Judgment, when our marks would be announced, and we would be ranked in order of achievement. Some would receive prizes—if they completed all the work according to Madame's rigorous standards. Despite my low spirits, I desperately wanted to succeed. My play might have been a disaster, but I would show them all that *la petite Anglaise* had a brain and could shine with the best of them.

In fact, no one in the cast of *Cleopatra* thought the performance had gone badly. The girls described our *grand spectacle* in glowing terms and once again, my *fête* was the talk of the schoolyard. I wished they would all just forget about it. Although Solange did her best to appear bored by their prattle, I saw the hurt look in her eyes.

Outside of school, I seemed to do nothing but say goodbye. We went to the Haywards for a last dinner. I bid Becky a tearful farewell; we promised to stay in touch. We'd grown very fond of the Haywards and felt at home in their exotic apartment. My father and big Berry plotted ways to work together in the future. My mother enjoyed Ruth's fierce intelligence. Frances and little Berry had formed a strong bond. That night Berry and Chris performed a little concert on recorder and flute for us. Becky presented me with a picture of the *Sacré Coeur* that she'd painted. All three planned to study with renowned masters of their various arts.

On *jeudi*, my father took me to the Tuileries to see a last puppet play. I did not pay much attention to the puppets. Instead, I gazed down the avenues of trees at the towering Palais du Louvre and watched the children sail boats around the sparkling fountain. It still felt magical to me, as though I'd stepped back in time. Only now I felt part of it, as though I could live here forever. I understood everything people said and spoke French as well as I spoke English.

I joined in a game of *marelle* (hopscotch) with Josée and Patrick after school. They welcomed me joyously, as though we'd never ceased playing together. When I won, they grinned and cheered.

"Are you really going away?" Josée asked, her eyes big and sad.

"Yes." I felt a lump in my throat. I wished I had spent more time with them. Why had I thought that because I'd made friends with the elite, I could no longer spend easy hours on the street with these two, who had welcomed me right from the start?

Madame Wax and Marie-Laurence invited us for a final visit. Madame clutched me and splotched my cheeks with kisses.

"I cannot bear for you to leave, *ma cherie.*" She gazed at me with tears in her eyes.

I smiled and wriggled out of her hot embrace.

"*Maman,*" said Marie-Laurence gently.

We perched on the overstuffed furniture in their apartment and listened to Madame giggle and chatter about

Marie-Laurence's success at university. Marie-Laurence looked uncomfortable.

We'd spent any number of evenings with them over the year. If Madame Wax had had her way, we'd have moved in with them, or at least I would have. My parents disliked visiting them, partly because the tiny flat felt so oppressive, partly because of Madame Wax's childish behaviour. Although my mother felt strongly that we should have them to our house and had issued repeated invitations, they'd almost always refused. We speculated that they would feel like interlopers in the *grand maison,* so agreed to visit their cramped home.

"She does love Meg and poor Marie-Laurence has been so kind," my mother said.

When we finally said good-bye, Madame cried and hugged me over and over again. Even Marie-Laurence seemed sad to see us go. My mother promised to write them with news of me.

We left feeling sorry for them. Madame Wax seemed like a little girl who'd never really grown up and only wanted another little girl to pet. Marie-Laurence, lonely, quiet and not terribly pretty, seemed trapped with her mother.

My mother had learned that Marie-Laurence's father was gone. Had he died? No one dared ask. My father thought maybe Madame had driven him away with her mindless chatter. Similarly, we hadn't been able to think of a way to ask why Marie-Laurence still lived at home. If she could not afford to live elsewhere, she never admitted it. Perhaps she realized her mother would not be able to cope alone. For a couple of years after our return to Canada, my mother and Marie-Laurence exchanged Christmas cards, with Madame always anxious for news of me. We hoped Marie-Laurence would one day manage to break free.

I meandered to and from school those last days, seeing the neighbourhood through nostalgic eyes. I knew every little shop so well. The proprietors greeted me with smiles. *"Comment ça va, petite?"* and *"Bonjour, Mademoiselle."* I chatted briefly; they felt like old friends. The *madame* at the *boulangerie* slipped me a free *pain au chocolate. "Merci beaucoup, Madame!"* I grinned at her.

Even the fierce *gendarme* with his little cape and cap no longer frightened me, though he did not smile. It seemed that policemen in France took their jobs terribly seriously, unlike the nice bobbies in England. The *gendarmes* stood like tin soldiers, directing traffic with straight-armed gestures and berating drivers who careened too close to them.

My final day of school dawned hot and perfectly clear. Along the boulevard, the sun streamed down through the tall trees with their skirts of iron grating. Dressed in a crisp pink dress and black patent leather shoes, my hair brushed to a shimmer, I skipped along with only the tiniest flutter in my tummy. *School's almost out!* I felt the familiar thrill at the thought of being free of the classroom for two whole months. But this time, my exuberance was tinged with sadness. In September, I'd dreaded starting school in a foreign country. I'd hated the little girls who looked down their noses at me or pointed and giggled. Now I saw a courtyard full of friends, all excited and chattering. In France, the last day did not consist of cookies and games. Today we would have a ceremony, at which awards would be granted. Everyone had dressed up. Even poor old Baggasin wore a clean dress, worn at the cuffs and too short for her, but clean. She did not speak to me but smiled in her vacant way. I returned the smile, remembering how she had befriended me when no one else would.

Solange arrived looking like a princess, in a royal blue dress with white flounces, sparkling barrettes in her dark gold hair. For a moment our eyes met. I looked away in discomfort, although she did not seem angry or hurt. Since my *fête*, she had adopted a neutral expression, neither friendly nor unfriendly, distant but apparently content. In some ways I wished she had returned to her old condescending manner. It would have been easy to get mad at her if she had.

We spent the morning rehearsing a poem we had to recite together. Madame beat out the tempo with her stick and upbraided us if we failed to put the emphasis on the correct word. She handed back our last assignments. I got 10 out of 10 on my arithmetic and 9 ½ on my *dictée*. Generously, she gave me a *Bon Point* for each. We all scrambled around in our desks, counting our *Bons Points* and our *Petite Images* to see if we had enough amassed to obtain the next level of award. I had hoped to get another *Grand Image* before year's end, but even after turning in my ten *Bon Points* for another *Petite Image,* I only had nine *Petite Images*. Still, only a few other girls had as many *Images* as I did, of any kind. Unlike the other girls, I did not crane to see the pictures that covered Solange's desk, many of them *Grande*. Once, she'd have delighted in showing them to me.

"*Margarette,*" whispered Sylvie, "You have so many. Perhaps you will win the *prix d'or.*"

I smiled. "No. We all know who will win the *prix d'or.*" Once I had hoped I might win it, just to show Solange. I'd imagined the look of chagrin on her face when Madame said *my* name, when I'd marched up to receive whatever it was

the winner received. Way down, I still wished I could out-
shine everyone, to prove how wrongheaded they had been
about me. Mostly I just hoped I would win *something*.

I had no appetite at lunch and gave half of my sandwich
to Sylvie, who always ate heartily. We leaned against the wall
of the school, not wanting to dirty our dresses by sitting on
the ground. Older girls carried out chairs for the expected
audience of parents. Madame called us back into the classroom and lectured us about how to behave.

"There will be no talking in the courtyard. You will line up
right outside the classroom." She jabbed a long finger at the
wall, as if we might get confused about the location of our
room. "You will stay still and wait patiently. You will not run
to visit with your families or make any other disturbances!"

We filed out into the sunshine. Girls of various ages
stood grouped in their classes around the courtyard. My
parents sat chatting to Solange's. My mother glanced up
and waved at me. I gave the tiniest shake of my head to let
her know this sort of exchange was not appropriate. I'm not
sure she understood; she simply returned her attention to
Solange's *maman*.

I grew increasingly nervous. It would be unbearable if I
did not receive any kind of recognition, yet I felt no certainty
that I would. How did they calculate such things? Although
I had done very well recently, in the first few months I had
failed miserably in practically every subject. I chewed on
my lip as the ceremony commenced. I couldn't stand the
thought of being embarrassed again.

Each class had its moment, beginning with the youngest.
The class stepped forward and sang a song or recited a poem.
The rest of us clapped politely and briefly. We wanted to get

on with it. Then the pertinent *maîtresse* spoke a few words of *félicitations* to the group before awarding the three top prizes: the *prix de bronze*, the *prix d'argent* and the *prix d'or*. Never having watched the Olympics, the precious metal names of the prizes reminded me of the fairy tale in which three dogs guarded an entrance, with eyes of bronze, silver and gold respectively. Some of the *maîtresses* seemed quite friendly; they actually smiled at the girls as they handed them their prizes, which were not bronze, silver or gold, but books—of medium size for the bronze, large for the silver and massive for the gold.

The entire courtyard seemed to hold its breath as the *maîtresse* announced the award winners and the girls in the class cheered and surrounded the winners, but only for a moment; then their *maîtresse* shushed them as the next *maîtresse* moved to the podium.

Our class came third. My stomach twisted as our dour Madame stalked forward, all long bony limbs and severe angles. She beckoned us forward with a sharp motion and we dutifully recited our poem while she frowned. Then she briefly commended us for working hard but could not refrain from mentioning that some girls had not met the standard and would not be progressing to the next grade. I glanced at Baggassin, whose usually blank face crumpled. I felt sorry for her. I doubted her parents had come to the ceremony. In fact, there were not nearly enough parents in the courtyard for the number of girls.

"*Le prix de bronze*," Madame announced, "is awarded to Danielle LeClerc."

Danielle, all smiles, tripped up to receive her book. I swallowed. Danielle was an excellent student, almost as good as

Solange. If she had won the prix de bronze, chances were I would win nothing.

"Le prix d'argent." She paused, looking at the paper in front of her, then raised her head to speak to the audience. "The winner of the silver prize has overcome many obstacles this year." She looked a bit sour. "It is awarded to Margarette Vestlay." She'd never been able to pronounce my last name.

The girls gasped audibly. It was the sweetest sound I'd ever heard. I marched forward and Madame handed me a large picture book and said, as if at great cost to herself, *"Félicitations."*

"Merci, Madame," I murmured, glancing out at my beaming parents.

Madame barely paused. "And I am pleased to bestow the *prix d'or* on one of the finest students in the entire school, Solange Dupuis."

Solange stepped forward, beautiful in her blue dress, her head held high, to receive a book the size of a world atlas. Madame's face softened for a second as she spoke to Solange.

The class erupted in cheers and rushed to embrace all three of us, but especially Solange, who received their accolades with smiling grace.

We returned to our place against the wall and I peeked in my book. It was, to my delight, a book of French Kings and Queens, gorgeously illustrated. I didn't know what I wanted to do more, peruse the book or bask in the glory of my success. As I glanced around, I caught sight of Baggasin, on the outskirts of our class group. A tear slipped down her cheek. Poor thing, she had almost certainly failed the year. I wondered what her first name might be. I'd never asked, and no one ever called her anything but Baggasin. She looked up and met my gaze. I gave her a little beckoning nod. Her eyes widened, and when I smiled, she shuffled past the other girls until she stood at my side. I opened my book to show her the pictures, no longer caring what the other girls thought. They didn't even seem to notice, but Baggasin grinned ear to ear.

When the ceremony ended, finally, I patted Baggasin's arm and said, *"Bonne Chance."* She just looked confused. Then Sylvie appeared and threw her arms around me. I stroked Sylvie's lovely hair as she examined my prize. Then we said good-bye and hugged a final time.

As I moved towards my parents, Solange intercepted me.

"Félicitations, Margarette," she said with a shy smile. "I am so glad for you."

My eyes filled with tears. Blinking them back, I congratulated her.

"May I see your book?" she asked tentatively.

I nodded and held it out so she could see.

"It is very beautiful." She gazed at it a moment and then asked, "Would you like to see mine?"

"Very much," I said. The sun shone down on us; I forgot about everyone else, Madame, my parents, Sylvie, Danielle.

Solange held out her book. The weight of it surprised me; I almost dropped it.

Solange made a funny face. "It is a bit excessive, is it not?"

I grinned, then looked down at the book. It was a History of the Ancient World. "It is *incroyable.*"

"There is a picture of Cleopatra," said Solange.

"No!" I laughed.

She opened the book to show me. The picture did not look at all like Elizabeth Taylor. "Yes," said Solange. "When I look at it, I will remember you."

Our eyes met, as we stood in a halo of golden light.

"I am so sorry, Solange," I said.

She gazed at me a moment longer, then gave that little shrug I loved which meant *it doesn't matter* and slipped her arm through mine. "Madame looked as though she might choke when she gave you the *prix d'argent,* did she not?"

We giggled. I looked over at the chairs. My parents and Solange's *maman* and *papa* stood watching us, frozen like statues. Then one by one their faces lit up in foolish smiles. Solange and I burst out laughing.

Epilogue

We spent the summer in the southwest of France with family friends from Montreal, in a villa high above the crashing surf of the Atlantic. It passed all too quickly. I recall almost nothing of the journey home. Perhaps, sunburnt and sleepy from my summer on the beach, I drifted all the way across the Atlantic in a dream.

I awoke with a jolt when we got home. Montreal West seemed bland and empty compared to France. The box-like stores that sold everything had none of the charm of the little shops in Paris. Our house with its big square porch and the hollyhocks in the back yard felt warm and familiar, but a little dull.

My tuberculosis was completely under control. I'd gained some weight. I no longer needed to rest all the time, but I felt uneasy about contacting my old school friends. It had been so long. I sat on the front porch in the late summer and thought about Solange. Soon school would start, and she would waltz into the cobbled schoolyard, but I would not.

Before we had left for France, my mother obtained an agreement from the school principal in Montreal West that I could enter Grade 4 upon my return. She'd anticipated I might be put back a year in Paris, as turned out to be the case. I'd been horrified at having to repeat a grade in France, but at least I would not have that embarrassing experience here. I would rejoin my old classmates.

My mother now had other ideas. She marched in to see the principal and declared, with something like outrage, that the French school system was vastly superior to our Canadian one and she thought I was now so advanced I should actually enter Grade 5. I wondered, for the first time, if it might have been preferable *not* to win the *prix d'argent*. The principal looked dubious; this was not the way things were done, but my mother persisted. Eventually, to my disgust, they had me write some tests. Upon reviewing the results, they grudgingly admitted I seemed to have sufficient knowledge to enter Grade 5.

This move felt awkward. In Paris I'd been playing with girls a year younger than me; now my classmates were a year older and showed a frightening level of sophistication. They scoffed at dolls. Instead they mooned over boys! I had a disturbing sense of *déjà vu* as the girls made fun of my naivety. I also struggled with schoolwork, at least for the first few months. I had, after all, missed two years of Canadian schooling and my finesse with a nib pen was meaningless in a world of ballpoints.

But I could speak perfect French, and that language now featured on the curriculum. On the first day I responded to every question the teacher posed in French and even kindly corrected her pronunciation a few times (she obviously was not French herself.) She did not take this well; in fact, she responded almost as negatively to my perfect French as *Madame* had to my inability to speak a word. She mocked me and spoke sarcastically about how Meg knew everything. I felt humiliated. Again. But I had learned a few lessons in Paris. I stopped answering questions and when I did, I made deliberate errors. Soon everyone forgot I knew French. Within a year my memory of the language had begun to fade. But I never forgot Paris, and the year I played the role of Margarette. If I shut my eyes I can see the shop windows at Christmas filled with tiny moving figures, the marionettes bashing each other in the puppet theatres in the Tuileries, Josée and Patrick waiting for me on the street corner, Sylvie spewing pearls and diamonds as we enacted *Les Fées,* poor old Bagassin sniffling and gazing at me with hopeful eyes. In my mind, I walk the narrow *rues* and wide *boulevards,* thick with the city's strange odours. I nod to the *madame* in the *boulangerie,* munch on fragrant *baguettes,* struggle with *resumés,* and race to the schoolyard to meet my friends in their *tabliers.* I watch Cleopatra entering Rome robed in gold. Above all I see Solange, winking, shrugging, grinning at me.

I wonder if she remembers her *petite amie anglaise.*

My father, me, Madame Wax and my mother

Me and Frances, in the Room With A View

Acknowledgements

I would like to thank all those who read early drafts of the book and provided me with invaluable feedback and encouragement—in particular members of the Stratford Writers Group circa 2010–2012 and the Deadly Prose online writers' group. Special thanks to David Pratt and Kathy McArthur for proof-reading the manuscript.

I am also deeply grateful to my parents for providing me with this unforgettable life experience.

About the Author

By the time she reached adulthood, Meg Westley had lived abroad for three years (one in Paris, two in South Wales) and travelled extensively in Europe. A PhD in Drama, she has worked as a stage manager, professor, coach, writer and editor. Passionate about education and human rights, she served as a school board trustee for 10 years and president of Dying With Dignity Canada for three. Her first novel *Goddess Fire* was published in 2009. Meg lives in Stratford, Canada and has written plays for children, short stories, academic articles, a monthly newspaper column, a blog (meg-westley.wordpress.com). Her favourite pastimes are playing Dungeons and Dragons, hiking, writing, and travelling.